How Living Things Function

HOUGHTON MIFFLIN

BOSTON

Printed in the U.S.A.   ISBN-13: 978-0-547-06244-0   ISBN-10: 0-547-06244-3   5 6 7 8 9-0868-16 15 14 13 12 11
4500278493

You Can...

Do What Scientists Do

Meet Dr. Paula Mikkelsen. She works at the American Museum of Natural History in New York City. She is in charge of the museum's collection of mollusks. The collection includes clamshells, snail shells, and the remains of slugs and squids. Dr. Mikkelsen helps other scientists find the mollusks they want to study.

Scientists ask questions. Then they answer them by investigating and experimenting.

In the Florida Keys, Dr. Mikkelsen has found 1,700 kinds of ocean mollusks. That number surprised her. It is three times the number other scientists predicted.

Dr. Mikkelsen has many questions about mollusks. For example, she wants to know how many kinds of mollusks live in the ocean around islands called the Florida Keys. To find out, she scuba dives to collect mollusks.

Back at the museum, Dr. Mikkelsen records the name of each new mollusk. Like all scientists, she keeps careful records of science information, or **data.**

Science investigations take many forms.

Dr. Mikkelsen collects animals to analyze. Other scientists make observations. Still others carry out experiments. Dr. Mikkelsen shares what she discovers with other scientists. They ask her questions about her data. Dr. Mikkelsen also shares her results with people in charge of protecting Florida wildlife. This helps them make decisions about how much scuba diving, boating, and fishing they can allow around the Keys.

Dr. Paula Mikkelsen uses tools such as these magnifying goggles to observe tiny mollusk shells.

Think Like a
Scientist

The ways scientists ask and answer questions about the world around them is called **scientific inquiry.** Scientific inquiry requires certain attitudes, or ways of thinking. To think like a scientist you have to be:

- curious and ask a lot of questions.

- creative and think up new ways to do things.

- willing to listen to the ideas of others but reach your own conclusions.

- open to change what you think when your investigation results surprise you.

- willing to question what other people tell you.

What attracts the bee to the flower? Is it color, odor, or something else?

Use Critical Thinking

When you think critically you make decisions about what others tell you or what you read. Is what you heard or read fact or opinion? A *fact* can be checked to make sure it is true. An *opinion* is what you think about the facts.

Did anyone ever tell you a story that was hard to believe? When you think, "That just can't be true," you are thinking critically. Critical thinkers question what they hear or read in a book.

It looks like bees are attracted to certain flowers. I wonder if they use color, smell, or something else, to tell one flower from another?

I read that bees are attracted to flowers by their smell, but they identify different flowers by their color and shape.

Science Inquiry

Applying scientific inquiry helps you understand the world around you. Say you have decided to keep Triops, or tadpole shrimp.

Observe You watch the baby Triops swim around in their tank. You notice how they swim.

Ask a Question When you think about what you saw, heard, or read you may have questions.

Hypothesis Think about facts you already know. Do you have an idea about the answer? Write it down. That is your hypothesis.

Experiment Plan a test that will tell if the hypothesis is true or not. List the materials you will need. Write the steps you will follow. Make sure that you keep all conditions the same except the one you are testing. That condition is called the *variable.*

Conclusion Think about your results. What do they tell you? Did your results support your hypothesis or show it to be false?

Describe your experiment to others. Communicate your results and conclusion. You can use words, charts, or graphs.

My Triops Experiment

Observe Light appears to cause Triops to change how they move.

Ask a Question I wonder, do Triops like to swim more in the daytime or the nighttime?

Hypothesis If I watch the Triops in dim light and then in bright light they will move differently.

Experiment I'm going to observe how the Triops move in dim light. Then I'm going to turn on a light and observe any changes.

Conclusion When I turn on a bright light, the Triops speed up in the water. The results support my hypothesis. Triops are more active in bright light than in dim light.

Inquiry Process

Here is a process that some scientists follow to answer questions and make new discoveries.

Make Observations

↓

Ask Questions

↓

Hypothesize

↓

Do an Experiment

↓

Draw a Conclusion

Hypothesis is Supported   **Hypothesis is Not Supported**

Science Inquiry Skills

You'll use many of these inquiry skills when you investigate and experiment.

- Ask Questions
- Observe
- Compare
- Classify
- Predict
- Measure

- Hypothesize
- Use Variables
- Experiment
- Use Models
- Communicate
- Use Numbers

- Record Data
- Analyze Data
- Infer
- Collaborate
- Research

Try It Yourself!

Experiment With a Matter Masher

To use the Matter Masher, put foam cubes or mini marshmallows in the bottle and screw on the cap. Then, push the top part of the cap up and down to pump air into the bottle.

1. Make a list of questions you have about the Matter Masher.

2. Think about how you could find out the answers.

3. Describe your experiment. If you did your experiment, what do you think the results would be?

You Can...

Be an Inventor

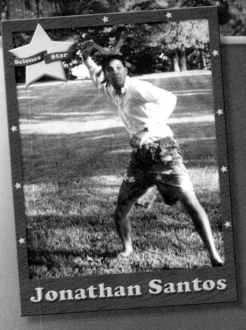

Jonathan Santos

His invention earned him his own trading card!

Jonathan Santos has been an inventor all his life. His first invention was a system of strings he used to switch off the lights without getting out of bed.

As a teenager, Jonathan invented a throwing toy called the J-Boom. He read about boomerangs. Then he planned his own toy with four arms instead of two. He built a sample, tried it out, and made improvements. Then he sold it in science museum gift shops.

Today, Jonathan works as a computer software engineer. He invents new ways to use computers. Jonathan is still inventing toys. His latest idea is a new kind of roller coaster!

"As a kid I quickly discovered that by using inventiveness you can design things and build things by using almost anything."

J·Boom

What Is Technology?

The tools people make and use and the things they build with tools are all **technology.** A wooden flying toy is technology. So is a space shuttle.

Scientists use technology, too. For example, a microscope makes it possible for them to see things that cannot be seen with just the eyes. They also use measurement tools to make their observations more exact.

Many technologies make the world a better place to live. But sometimes a technology that solves one problem can cause other problems. For example, riding in cars or buses makes it easier for people to travel long distances. But the fuel that powers cars and buses pollutes the air. Air pollution causes health problems for people and other living things.

A Better Idea

"I wish I had a better way to _____". How would you fill in the blank? Everyone wishes they could find a way to do their jobs more easily or have more fun. Inventors try to make those wishes come true. Inventing or improving an invention requires time and patience.

Many inventors have improved video game controllers. Maybe, someday, you will invent a new way to play video games.

Video Game Controller

joystick

buttons to choose actions

direction button

How to Be an Inventor

1. **Identify a problem.** It may be a problem at school, at home, or in your community.

2. **List ways to solve the problem.** Sometimes the solution is a new tool. Other times it may be a new way of doing an old job or activity.

3. **Choose the best solution.** Decide which idea will work best. Think about which one you can carry out.

4. **Make a sample.** A sample, called a *prototype,* is the first try. Your idea may need many materials or none at all. Choose measuring tools that will help your design work better.

5. **Try out your invention.** Use your prototype or ask some else to try it. Keep a record of how it works and what problems you find.

6. **Improve your invention.** Use what you learned to make your design work better. Draw or write about the changes you made and why you made them.

7. **Share your invention.** Show your invention to others. Explain how it works. Tell how it makes an activity easier or more fun. If it did not work as well as you wanted, tell why.

You Can...

Make Decisions

Troubles for Baby Turtles

Each spring adult female sea turtles come out of the ocean in the dark of night. They crawl onto sandy beaches and dig nest holes. They lay their eggs, cover them with sand, and slip back into the ocean.

A few weeks later, and all at once, the babies hatch and climb out of the nest. Attracted to nature's bright lights, the turtles should crawl toward the lights of the night sky shining on the ocean. But on many beaches, the lights from streetlights or houses are much brighter. The baby turtles crawl away from the ocean and toward the electric lights. Instead of finding their home in the sea, many of them die.

Deciding What to Do

How could you help save the most baby turtles?

Here's how to make your decision about the baby turtles. You can use the same steps to help solve problems in your home, in your school, and in your community.

Learn → Learn about the problem. Take the time needed to get the facts. You could talk to an expert, read a science book, or explore a web site.

List → Make a list of actions you could take. Add actions other people could take.

Decide → Think about each action on your list. Decide which choice is the best one for you or your community.

Share → Communicate your decision to others.

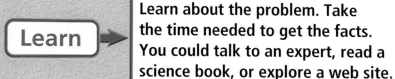

Science Safety

☑ Know the safety rules of your school and classroom and follow them.

☑ Read and follow the safety tips in each Investigation activity.

☑ When you plan your own investigations, write down how to keep safe.

☑ Know how to clean up and put away science materials. Keep your work area clean and tell your teacher about spills right away.

☑ Know how to safely plug in electrical devices.

☑ Wear safety goggles when your teacher tells you.

☑ Unless your teacher tells you to, never put any science materials in or near your ears, eyes, or mouth.

☑ Wear gloves when handling live animals.

☑ Wash your hands when your investigation is done.

Caring for Living Things

☑ Learn how to care for the plants and animals in your classroom so that they stay healthy and safe. Learn how to hold animals carefully.

LIFE SCIENCE

UNIT A

How Living Things Function

How Living Things Function

Independent Reading

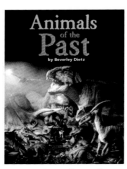

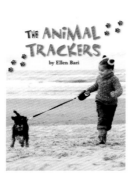

**Animals of
the Past**

**The Animal
Trackers**

**Follow Me,
Be a Bee**

Discover!

Dolphins and people differ in some ways. Dolphins have fins and flippers. People have arms and legs. But dolphins and people are alike in some ways. What traits do dolphins and people have in common? You will have the answer to this question by the end of the unit.

Chapter 1

Parts of Plants

Lesson Preview

LESSON 1

Carrots, radishes, turnips, and beets— what part of a plant are these vegetables?

Read about it in Lesson 1.

LESSON 2

Leaves, roots, and stems—how can these parts be used to identify plants?

Read about it in Lesson 2.

LESSON 3

From seeds in a tasty fruit to leaves shaped so they hold water—how do parts of plants help them survive in different environments?

Read about it in Lesson 3.

How Do Plants Use Their Parts?

Why It Matters...

Plants are living things that people use for many purposes. If you have ever enjoyed the shade of a tree on a warm day, then you have used plants. Plants provide people with food to eat, material for clothing and buildings, and many other items.

PREPARE TO INVESTIGATE

Inquiry Skill

Observe When you observe, you gather information about the environment using your senses of sight, hearing, smell, and touch.

Materials

- bean seed
- plastic bag with seal
- stapler
- paper towels
- water
- hand lens
- masking tape
- metric ruler

Science and Math Toolbox

For steps 2 and 3, review **Using a Hand Lens** on page H2.

Bean Bags
Procedure

STEP 1

1 **Collaborate** Work with a partner. Wet a paper towel until it is damp, but not dripping. Fold the paper towel and slide it into a plastic bag, as shown. Staple the bag about 2 cm from the bottom. Use a ruler to help you measure.

STEP 2

2 **Observe** Look closely at a bean seed with your hand lens. In your *Science Notebook*, draw a picture of the bean seed. Label the picture *Day 1.* Place the bean seed in the bag. Seal the bag.

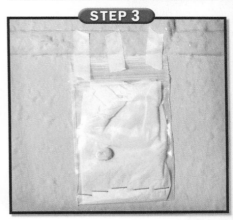

STEP 3

3 **Observe** Tape the bag so it hangs in a sunny spot. Use your hand lens to observe the bean seed each day. Draw and label a picture of the bean seed each day. Add water as needed to keep the paper towel damp.

4 **Research** After you have observed a change in the bean seed, use library books or the Internet to learn how to plant the bean seed in soil and care for it.

Conclusion

1. **Classify** Would you say that a bean seed is a living thing? Why or why not?

2. **Infer** Based on your observations, what does a bean seed need in order to sprout?

Investigate More!

Design an Experiment
Use scissors to cut off a small part of the bean plant. Use a hand lens to observe and draw the changes to the plant every day.

Plants Meet Their Needs

VOCABULARY

cell	p. A8
leaf	p. A8
nutrient	p. A7
plant	p. A6
root	p. A8
stem	p. A8

READING SKILL

Text Structure Read the headings at the top of each section. Write down an idea that you think you will read about in each section.

MAIN IDEA Plants use their parts to meet their basic needs.

Plants

Living things, or things that are alive, are found all over Earth. All of the living things on Earth can be separated into groups. Two groups of living things are plants and animals. A **plant** is a living thing that grows on land or in the water, cannot move from place to place, and usually has green leaves.

These sunflowers need sunlight and air to grow. They also need water and nutrients from soil.

The Needs of Plants

Humans and other animals need air to breathe, water to drink, and food to eat. Plants need certain things to live too. They need water, air, and sunlight. Most plants also need soil, which provides nutrients (NOO tree-uhnts). A **nutrient** is a substance that living things need to survive and grow.

▶ **TEXT STRUCTURE** What subheadings could have been used in the section called *The Needs of Plants*?

sunlight

water

air

soil

Parts of Plants

Like animals and all other living things, plants are made of cells (sehlz). A **cell** is the smallest and most basic unit of a living thing. Plant cells have stiff walls that support the plant and give it shape.

Plants cannot move from place to place to find food and water like animals can. So how do plants meet their needs? They have parts that help them get the things they need to stay alive.

Almost all plants have three parts. Each part does a job that helps the plant live. A **root** takes in water and nutrients and provides support for the plant. A **stem** holds up the leaves and carries water and nutrients through the plant. A **leaf** collects sunlight and gases from the air. It uses them to make food for the plant.

The zebra plant is unusual because it has leaves patterned like zebra fur. What features does it have in common with other plants? ▶

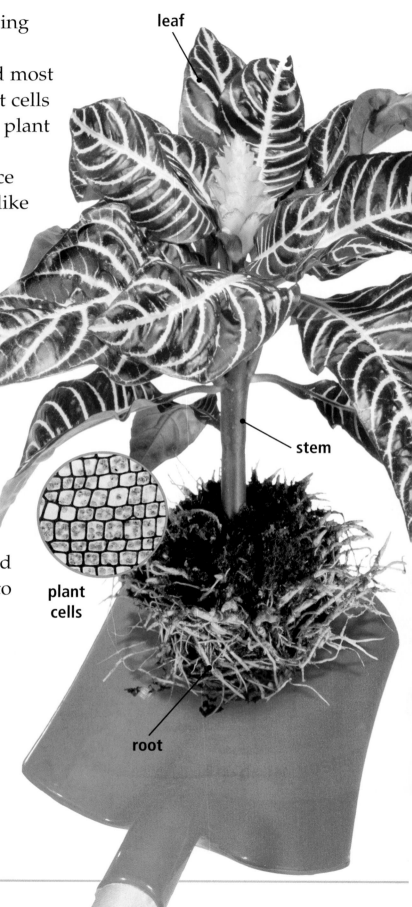

leaf

stem

plant cells

root

Roots

You usually don't see the roots of a plant. The roots of most plants grow underground. The most important job of roots is to take in water and nutrients from the soil. Roots have tiny hairlike parts that help them do this.

The roots of most plants also have another job. Roots are needed to hold the plant in place in the soil and to help it stand up. Tall trees have huge roots that help keep them from tipping over. Roots of grasses help hold them in place.

Sometimes, roots store food for the plant. The carrots you eat are actually roots. They contain many nutrients that they store for use by the whole carrot plant. Radishes, turnips, beets, and some other vegetables that people eat are also roots.

▶ **TEXT STRUCTURE** If page A8 ended after the first paragraph, what would be a better head for that page?

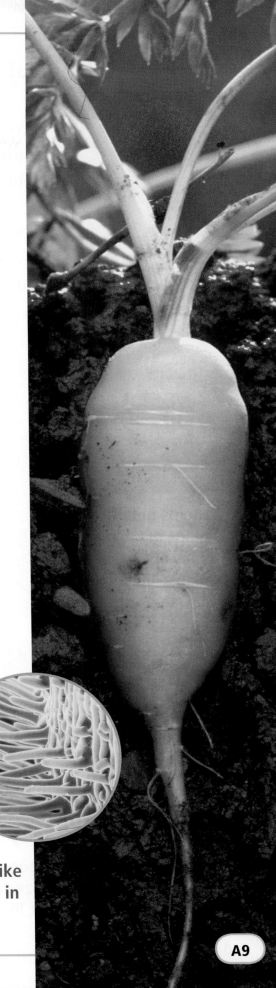

Root hairs viewed through a microscope ▶

Carrots are roots. They have tiny hairlike parts, called root hairs, that help take in water and nutrients from soil. ▶

Stems

The stems of many plants are long and thin. They contain small tubes. These tubes carry water and nutrients throughout the plant. The stems hold up the leaves. This allows the leaves to collect sunlight.

Some stems, such as the stems of sugar cane, can store food. In a cactus plant, the stems store water. Tree trunks are also stems. Celery stalks and asparagus are examples of stems eaten by people.

▲ Stems help a plant grow tall. These bamboo plants have long, strong stems that grow very quickly.

This Japanese maple bonsai (bahn SY) is a tiny form of a full-size tree. It has roots, stems, and leaves, just like a large tree. ▶

Leaves

Leaves grow out of the stem of a plant. Most plants have many leaves. The leaf is the part of the plant that makes food. Leaves take in sunlight and air, and use them to make sugar. The sugar is food for the plant.

Leaves usually grow near the top of the plant so they can take in a lot of sunlight. Different types of plants usually have differently shaped leaves. The spines on a cactus are leaves. So are the needles of a pine tree. You might eat the leaves of some plants, such as lettuce, spinach, or cabbage.

▶ **TEXT STRUCTURE** Look back at the last three heads in this lesson. What are the three parts of a plant?

▲ This Japanese maple leaf is divided into sections called lobes.

This plant is called a ponytail palm. Its leaves are long and narrow. ▶

How Plants Meet Needs

The roots, stems, and leaves of a plant are all connected. They work together to help the plant meet its needs. To live and grow, a plant must meet its needs. Roots take in water and nutrients from soil. Stems carry the water and nutrients to the leaves and other parts of the plant. Leaves use sunlight, water, and air to make sugar.

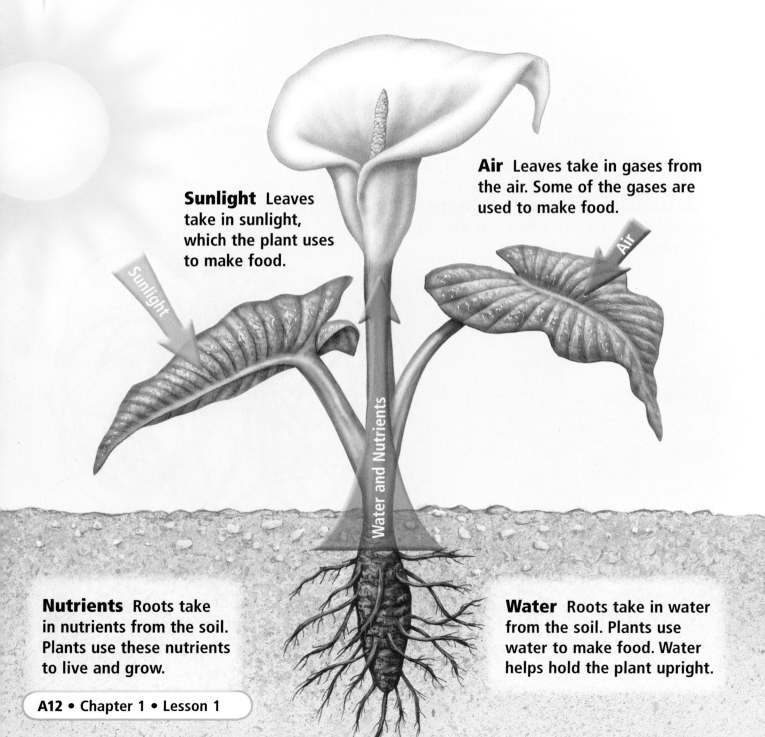

Sunlight Leaves take in sunlight, which the plant uses to make food.

Air Leaves take in gases from the air. Some of the gases are used to make food.

Nutrients Roots take in nutrients from the soil. Plants use these nutrients to live and grow.

Water Roots take in water from the soil. Plants use water to make food. Water helps hold the plant upright.

Lesson Wrap-Up

Visual Summary

 Plants need air, water, sunlight, and nutrients to live.

 Plants have roots, stems, and leaves and are made of cells.

 The roots, stems, and leaves of a plant work together to help the plant meet its needs.

LINKS for Home and School

MATH Add It Up A rabbit eats 2 celery stalks, 2 carrots, 3 radishes, 1 turnip, and 1 head of lettuce. How many vegetables does the rabbit eat in all? How many of the vegetables eaten are roots?

HEALTH Make a Poster Native Americans used the bark of willow trees as a pain medicine. Today, chemicals found in willow bark are used to make aspirin. Many modern medicines come from parts of plants. Make a poster listing some common modern medicines. Include drawings of the plants they are made from.

Review

❶ **MAIN IDEA** How does a plant meet its needs?

❷ **VOCABULARY** What is the job of roots?

❸ **READING SKILL: Text Structure** Which heading would most likely have information about root structure: *Parts of Plants* or *Needs of Plants*?

❹ **CRITICAL THINKING: Synthesize** Describe how stems and leaves of a plant work to help the plant live.

❺ **INQUIRY SKILL: Observe** Suppose a plant has plenty of light, soil, and air. Its leaves are turning brown and dry. Which of its needs is not being met?

 TEST PREP
The main job of leaves is to ___.

A. hold up the plant.

B. make food for the plant.

C. take in water and nutrients.

D. store food for the plant.

 Technology
Visit **www.eduplace.com/scp/** to find out more about the needs of plants.

result
result
result
A13

How Do Parts Help Classify Plants?

Why It Matters...

There are over 300,000 kinds of plants! Plants vary greatly in how they look. You can use plant parts to tell one type of plant from another. It is helpful to be able to tell different types of plants apart. For example, you must be able to identify plants to use them safely for food and medicine.

PREPARE TO INVESTIGATE

Inquiry Skill

Communicate You can present science information using numbers, words, sketches, charts, and graphs.

Materials

- leaves
- hand lens

Science and Math Toolbox

For step 2, review **Using a Hand Lens** on page H2.

Leaf Detective
Procedure

1 **Communicate** In your *Science Notebook*, make a diagram like the one shown.

2 **Observe** Examine some leaves using a hand lens. Observe the size, shape, color, and texture of each leaf.

3 **Classify** First, group the leaves by size. Divide the leaves into two groups, small and large. Write these group names in your diagram. Write one group name in each box below the word *Leaves*.

4 **Classify** Work only with the small leaves. Classify the small leaves into two groups based on something other than size. Name each group. Write these group names in your diagram. Write one name in each box below the word *Small*.

5 **Classify** Repeat step 4 to further classify the large leaves.

Conclusion

1. **Collaborate** Compare your diagram with a classmate's diagram. How are they alike? How are they different?

2. **Analyze Data** What is one leaf trait that you used to group the leaves? Did your classmate also use that trait?

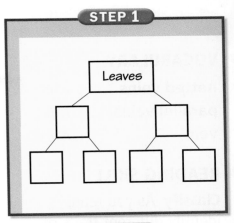

STEP 1

STEP 2

STEP 3

Investigate More!

Research Collect a few tree leaves. Ask a librarian for a field guide book to trees or use a guide on the Internet. Use the field guide to help you find the name of the tree each leaf came from.

Classifying Plants

VOCABULARY

netted veins   p. A16
parallel veins   p. A16
vein   p. A16

READING SKILL

Classify As you read, identify different traits of roots, stems, and leaves.

MAIN IDEA Plants can be classified by the different traits of their leaves, stems, and roots.

Classifying by Leaves

One way that scientists classify, or group, plants is by their leaves. Leaves can be classified by the shape of their outside edge, called the leaf margin. Leaves can also be classified by their texture or by the pattern of their veins (vaynz).

A **vein** is a tube that carries food, water, and nutrients throughout a leaf. Leaves can have parallel veins or netted veins. **Parallel veins** are veins that run in straight lines next to each other. **Netted veins** are veins that branch out from main veins.

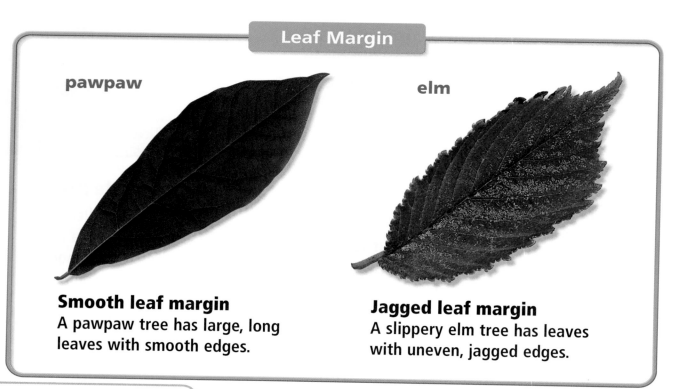

Leaf Margin

pawpaw

elm

Smooth leaf margin
A pawpaw tree has large, long leaves with smooth edges.

Jagged leaf margin
A slippery elm tree has leaves with uneven, jagged edges.

jade

cucumber

sassafras

Waxy texture
Jade plants have leaves with a waxy surface. This helps keep the plant from drying out.

Rough texture
Cucumber plants have leaves with a rough texture.

Smooth texture
Sassafras (SAS uh fras) plants have smooth, shiny, green leaves.

Vein Pattern

corn

grape

Parallel veins
Corn leaves have long veins that run next to one another.

Netted veins
Grape leaves have a pattern of veins with many branches.

 **CLASSIFY** What are three ways to classify leaves?

Classifying by Stems and Roots

Plants can also be classified by their stem structures and root systems. Stems are either woody or soft. A root system is all of the roots of a single plant. Root systems are made up of either a taproot or fibrous (FY bruhs) roots. A taproot is a thick single root. Fibrous roots are small roots that spread out over a wide area.

Stem Structure

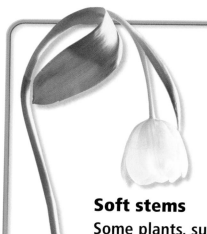

Woody stems
Bushes, such as this holly, and most trees, have hard, woody stems. Woody stems are protected by bark.

Soft stems
Some plants, such as tulips, have soft stems. These stems are held up by water inside their tubes.

Root Systems

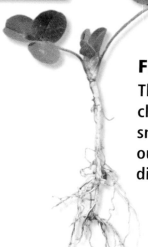

Taproots
A dandelion has a single long, thick root. Carrots are also taproots.

Fibrous roots
The roots of clover plants are small and branch out in different directions.

 **CLASSIFY** Name two kinds of root systems.

Visual Summary

	Leaves are classified by leaf margin, texture, and vein pattern.
	Stems can be classified as soft or woody.
	Root systems can be classified as taproots or fibrous roots.

LINKS for Home and School

MATH Make Shapes Collect leaves from different trees and plants. Make imprints of the leaves by dipping them in paint and pressing them against a sheet of paper. What geometric figures do you see? Look for and label any parallel lines and lines of symmetry.

WRITING Persuasive Plants can be classified by their parts and in other ways. Write a paragraph to persuade other people that classifying plants is important.

Review

❶ MAIN IDEA How are plants classified?

❷ VOCABULARY Write a definition for *veins* as it is used in this lesson.

❸ READING SKILL: Classify What are two kinds of roots? Give examples of plants that have each kind of root.

❹ CRITICAL THINKING: Evaluate If you found two leaves with the same leaf margin and vein pattern, could you conclude that they came from the same plant? Why or why not?

❺ INQUIRY SKILL: Communicate Draw a diagram that shows ways of classifying leaves.

✔ TEST PREP
Root systems are classified as either ___.

   A. smooth or rough.

   B. soft or woody.

   C. parallel or netted.

   D. taproots or fibrous.

 Technology
Visit **www.eduplace.com/scp/** to read more about classifying plants.

It's So Corny!

You might not see it, but corn is all around you. You probably used corn today. It's hard to avoid eating, wearing, or using something made from corn! There's corn in soap, lotion, shampoo, and toothpaste.

Cornstarch is a type of flour that is made from corn. The paper, books, rulers, chalk, paint, crayons, and erasers that you use at school are likely made with cornstarch. You can't read, write, or draw without corn.

Even when you are riding in a car, you might be using corn. Ethanol, which is made from corn, is sometimes added to gasoline. When the gasoline that is burned in a car engine contains ethanol, less pollution is produced. Corn really is everywhere!

Corn is used to produce threads in pillows, comforters, and carpeting.

The paste in wallpaper is made from cornstarch. This paste dries slowly.

Cornstarch helps keep crayons from breaking.

Sharing Ideas

1. **READING CHECK** What are three things that are made from corn?

2. **WRITE ABOUT IT** What are some ways that you used things made from corn today?

3. **TALK ABOUT IT** Discuss why corn is an important plant.

A21

How Do Their Parts Help Plants Survive?

Why It Matters...

Have you ever blown on a puffy, white dandelion? If so, you have seen its small pieces of fluff drift around in the air. Some of those pieces land on soil and produce new dandelions. All plants have parts that help them survive and grow new plants.

PREPARE TO INVESTIGATE

Inquiry Skill

Infer When you infer, you use facts you know and observations you have made to draw a conclusion.

Materials

- cactus
- hand lens
- tweezers
- plastic spoon

Science and Math Toolbox

For steps 2 and 3, review **Using a Hand Lens** on page H2.

Cactus Spine
Procedure

STEP 1

1. **Record Data** Work with a partner. In your *Science Notebook,* make a sketch of the cactus. Use tweezers to pull a spine off the cactus. **Safety:** Never touch a cactus. Cactus spines can be sharp.

2. **Observe** Look at the spine with a hand lens. The spine is a leaf of the cactus. Record your observations.

STEP 2

3. **Observe** Use a plastic spoon to gently move some of the soil around the base of the cactus. Use the spoon to remove a small amount of soil. Place the soil on a sheet of paper. Observe the soil with a hand lens. Record your observations.

4. Continue to move soil around the base of the cactus until you can see some roots. Sketch them in your *Science Notebook*. Note whether the roots grew deeply or were close to the surface of the soil.

STEP 4

5. **Analyze Data** On your sketch of the cactus, label its roots, stem, and leaves.

Conclusion

1. **Infer** Based on your observations, where do you think a cactus lives?

2. **Infer** How do the parts of a cactus help it survive where it lives?

Investigate More!

Solve a Problem In some dry places, people use large amounts of water for lawns. Many communities are trying to reduce water use. How could these people help save water?

▶ **READING SKILL**

Draw Conclusions
Identify some unusual features of a plant you read about. Draw a conclusion about that plant's environment.

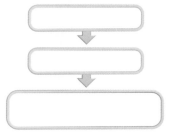

Ways to Meet Needs

MAIN IDEA Plants have parts that help them live in many different environments.

Getting and Storing Water

Plants grow in many kinds of environments (ehn VY ruhn muhnts). An **environment** is everything that surrounds and affects a living thing. Different plants have parts that help them survive in their environment.

Some plants in shady environments grow high on tree trunks. This allows the plants to reach sunlight. But their roots cannot reach the soil. The roots are able to take water from the air. Other plants, like cactuses, can store water to use at a later time.

◀ Orchids grow high on tree trunks. Their roots take in water from the air.

▲ A tank bromeliad stores up to 8 L (about 2 gal) of water between its leaves.

Root Support

Trees that live in warm, wet environments grow in soil that is often soft. Most of the nutrients in soil are near the surface. Trees that grow in such soil need wide, shallow roots for support and to take in nutrients.

Some types of trees have strong, woody roots called prop roots. Prop roots grow above the soil from the tree's trunk. They support the trunk in the wet ground.

Large trees need a lot of support. Some large trees have long, flattened roots called buttress roots. Buttress roots grow on the surface of the ground and widen the base of the tree. The widened base helps to hold up the tree.

▶ DRAW CONCLUSIONS **Draw a conclusion about what the air is like around plants that grow on tree trunks.**

▲ The buttress roots of a giant fig tree hold its huge trunk upright.

◀ Sturdy prop roots seem to hold these palm trees in midair.

Spreading Seeds

Most plants reproduce (ree pruh DOOS) using seeds. To **reproduce** means to make new living things of the same kind. A seed is the first stage of a new plant. To grow into a new plant, a seed must fall where there is enough sunlight, soil, and water. If it grows too close to the plant that produced it, a seed may not survive. The parent plant may take up most of the sunlight, soil, and water in the area.

Many seeds have parts that help them travel away from the parent plant. Some seeds travel on the wind, some float in water, and some hook onto the fur of animals. Some seeds are inside tasty fruit. Animals eat the fruit, leaving the seeds behind.

▶ **DRAW CONCLUSIONS** Draw conclusions about what may have prevented a seed from producing a healthy new plant.

▲ The shape of maple seeds causes them to twirl as they fall. The twirling helps the seeds travel farther away from the tree.

Burdock seeds hook onto the fur of passing animals. ▼

▲ Because coconut seeds float, they can drift on the ocean from island to island.

Visual Summary

Plants have parts that take in and store water in different ways.

Plants that grow in soft, wet soil have roots that help support them.

Plants spread seeds using wind, water, or animals.

LINKS for Home and School

MATH **Find the Number** There are coconut trees growing on an island. Use the following clues to find the number of fallen coconuts on the island. There is a 3 in the hundreds place. The digit in the tens place is less than 9 and greater than 7. The digit in the ones place is twice the digit in the hundreds place.

TECHNOLOGY **Make a List** Sometimes inventors get their ideas from observing plants and animals. Make a list of machines that may have been invented when an inventor saw maple seeds falling from a tree.

Review

① MAIN IDEA How are plants able to live in many different environments?

② VOCABULARY What is an *environment*?

③ READING SKILL: Draw Conclusions You see a plant that has thick, waxy skin and a stem that stores water. What kind of environment might this plant live in?

④ CRITICAL THINKING: Evaluate A friend says that he cannot grow a garden because his area is too dry. Respond to this idea.

⑤ INQUIRY SKILL: Infer What can you infer about how a seed with a parachute-shaped structure moves away from its parent plant?

✓ TEST PREP
Prop roots help a plant ___.

A. stand upright on wet soil.

B. make extra food.

C. store water in a dry environment.

D. spread seeds.

Technology
Visit **www.eduplace.com/scp/** to research more about plants in their environments.

Plants That Hunt

Gotcha! A fly smells some sweet sap. Looking for dinner, it crawls between two spiky leaves. Suddenly, the leaves snap shut. Instead of finding dinner, the bug becomes dinner. The Venus flytrap strikes again!

Most plants get enough nutrients from water and soil. The Venus flytrap, however, is a meat-eating, or carnivorous plant. Because it lives in places where the soil is poor, it adds to its diet by catching and digesting insects and other tiny creatures.

◄ **Sticky trap** A sundew leaf traps insects with sticky threads called tentacles. Then it folds up to digest its meal.

Danger! Keep out! ▶ Once inside this pitcher plant, insects slide down a slippery slope to a deadly pool. There the plant digests them, much as your stomach digests food.

A29

Vocabulary

Complete each sentence with a term from the list.

1. The part of a plant that makes food is called a/an _____.

2. Corn leaves have _____ that run in lines next to each other.

3. Everything that surrounds and affects a living thing is a/an _____.

4. Some leaves have _____ that branch out from main veins.

5. A substance that living things need to survive is a/an _____.

6. To make more living things of the same kind is to _____.

7. The part of most plants that grow underground is the _____.

8. A living thing that cannot move from place to place and usually has green leaves is a/an _____.

9. A tube that carries water and nutrients throughout a leaf is a/an _____.

10. The basic unit that makes up all living things is a/an _____.

cell A8
environment A24
leaf A8
netted veins A16
nutrient A7
parallel veins A16
plant A6
reproduce A26
root A8
stem A8
vein A16

Test Prep

Write the letter of the best answer choice.

11. The _____ of a plant holds up the leaves and carries water and nutrients to all parts of the plant.

   A. root system
   B. stem
   C. parallel vein
   D. leaf

12. Veins in a leaf can be _____.

   A. tap or fibrous.   C. smooth or rough.
   B. soft or woody.   D. parallel or netted.

13. Plants that grow on the trunks of trees have parts that help them get _____ from the air.

   A. water
   B. seeds
   C. roots
   D. food

14. Plants need water, soil, air, and _____.

   A. salt.   C. sunlight.
   B. seeds.   D. pots.

15. Communicate Make a sketch of a leaf that has either a smooth or jagged leaf margin and parallel or netted veins. Write a brief description of this leaf to explain your drawing.

16. Infer Leaves need to collect enough sunlight to make food. Suppose you see two plants. One has large, broad leaves. The other has small, narrow leaves. What can you infer about the amount of sunlight in the environment in which each plant lives?

Map the Concept

Fill in the concept map with the parts of a plant. You may use each term more than once.

root system   **root**
leaf   **stem**

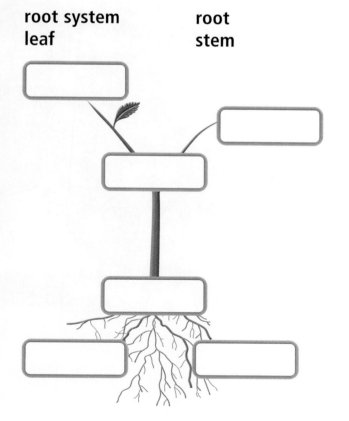

Critical Thinking

17. Apply Suppose you make a salad with the following vegetables: lettuce, celery, carrots, spinach and radishes. Classify each of these vegetables as a root, stem, or leaf.

18. Synthesize Imagine that you could change the parts of a cactus so that it could live in a wet, forest environment. What changes would you make to its roots, stems, and leaves?

19. Analyze If you cut off the roots of a plant, which of the plant's needs would no longer be met?

20. Evaluate Suppose you read an article that states that it is almost impossible to tell two particular plants apart. Their leaves and stems look exactly alike. How might you tell these plants apart?

Performance Assessment

Write Directions
Houseplants often come with cards that tell the buyer how to care for the plant. Write a set of directions telling someone how he or she could help a plant meet its needs.

Chapter 2

Classifying Animals

LESSON 1

From fish scales to bird feathers—how are animals with backbones classified?

Read about it in Lesson 1.

LESSON 2

Spiders, worms, and clams—what do these animals have in common?

Read about it in Lesson 2.

LESSON 3

Woolly mammoths and saber-toothed cats— are these animals similar to animals living today?

Read about it in Lesson 3.

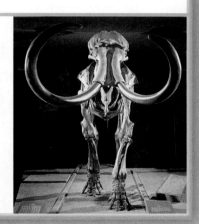

Which Animals Are Vertebrates?

Why It Matters...

When you pet a cat, you may feel hard bones along its back. What you are feeling is the cat's backbone. The backbone, and other bones, support the cat's body and give it shape. Most of the animals you know best have backbones. Your family and friends, dogs and cats, farm animals, fish, and even pigeons in the park have backbones.

PREPARE TO INVESTIGATE

Inquiry Skill

Use Models You can use a model of an object to better understand or describe how the real object works.

Materials

- pipe cleaner
- square beads
- plastic washers
- photo of snake
- photo of bird

Model a Backbone
Procedure

1. **Collaborate** Work with a partner to make a model of a backbone. A **backbone** is a series of bones that runs down the back of some animals.

STEP 2

2. **Use Models** Bend one end of a pipe cleaner so the beads will not slide off. Slide a bead, then a washer, onto the pipe cleaner.

STEP 3

3. **Use Models** String beads and washers until there is a small space left at the end of the pipe cleaner. Bend this end so the beads and washers do not slide off.

4. **Ask Questions** Examine pictures of a snake and a bird. Write one question in your *Science Notebook* about the shape of each animal's backbone.

STEP 4

5. **Communicate** Answer your question by bending your model to match each animal's backbone. Draw a picture of your model in your *Science Notebook*.

Conclusion

1. **Infer** How does a backbone that can bend help an animal to move?

2. **Predict** How might an animal's ability to move change if its backbone were rigid like a metal tube?

Investigate More!
Design an Experiment
Model another backbone. Place three small rubber bands between each bead. Bend the backbone to match the snake's backbone. How do the rubber bands change the way the backbone moves?

VOCABULARY

amphibian	p. A40
backbone	p. A36
bird	p. A38
fish	p. A39
mammal	p. A37
reptile	p. A41
vertebrate	p. A36

▶ READING SKILL

Classify Title one column *Animal* and the other column *Group.* For each animal, write the name of its group: robin, frog, alligator, rabbit, shark.

Classifying Vertebrates

MAIN IDEA Animals with backbones can be classified into groups according to their traits.

Traits of Vertebrates

You have learned that a plant is one type of living thing. An animal is another type. Like plants, animals are made of many cells. They can grow and change and they can reproduce. Unlike plants, animals eat food, and most animals can move from place to place.

Animals can be classified, or divided, into two groups depending on whether or not they have a backbone. A **backbone** is a series of bones that runs down the back of some animals. It helps to support the animal's body. An animal that has a backbone is called a **vertebrate** (VUR tuh briht). Most animals do not have a backbone.

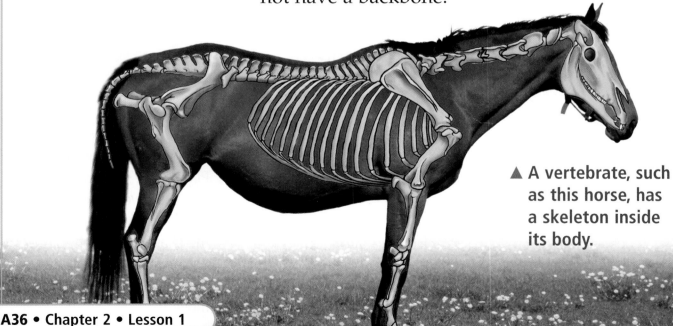

▲ A vertebrate, such as this horse, has a skeleton inside its body.

Mammals

Vertebrates can be classified into several smaller groups. One of these groups is the mammal (MAM uhl) group. A **mammal** is an animal that has hair or fur and produces milk for its young.

Mammals, like all animals, need oxygen, a gas in air, to live. Mammals breathe air with their lungs. Even mammals that live in water, such as whales, sea lions, and dolphins have lungs and must breathe air. These animals swim to the water's surface when they need to take a breath.

Most mammals have a thick coat of hair or fur that traps air against the body for warmth. Mammals with little hair on their body keep warm in other ways.

▲ **Humans are mammals.**

 **CLASSIFY** **What are two traits of mammals?**

Sea lions are mammals that live both in water and on land.

Birds

Another group of vertebrates is the bird group. A **bird** is a vertebrate that has feathers, lungs, wings, and two legs. Birds lay eggs that have hard shells. When the eggs hatch, most bird parents feed the young until they are strong enough to find their own food.

Most birds can fly. Strong muscles help a bird move its wings. Feathers keep a bird warm but are light so they do not weigh the bird down. Some of a bird's bones are hollow. Hollow bones make the bird lightweight so it can fly easily.

▲ Large wings, light feathers, and hollow bones help this owl to fly.

The strong beak of the puffin is used for catching and eating fish. ▼

▲ The Victoria Crowned Pigeon has a feathered crest.

sand tiger shark

Caribbean stingray

parrot fish

Fish

Fish are vertebrates that live in water. Many fish have long, narrow bodies that make it easy for them to move through water. Most fish are covered with scales—hard, thin, flat plates—that protect them and help them to swim. Scales are covered with a layer of slime which helps keep them waterproof. Fins keep the fish upright and help it steer through the water.

Like all animals, fish need oxygen to live. Fish do not have lungs. Instead, they have gills. Gills take oxygen gas from water. A fish breathes by taking water in through its mouth. The water is then pumped through the gills, which remove the oxygen.

▲ All fish have backbones. Sharks and rays have backbones made of cartilage (KAHR tih lihj), a material that is softer than bone.

 **CLASSIFY** What are two traits of fish?

Amphibians

An **amphibian** (am FIHB ee uhn) is a vertebrate that starts life in the water and then lives on land as an adult. Amphibians, such as frogs, toads, and salamanders, lay eggs in water. Young amphibians that hatch from the eggs look very different from adults. The young breathe with gills and have tails that help them swim.

As young amphibians grow, their bodies change. Lungs and legs develop, and their gills disappear. After the young amphibians' bodies change, they live on land and breathe air with their lungs.

▲ Toads, such as this Malagasy painted toad, have rough, dry, bumpy skin.

Frogs have wet, smooth skin. Wet skin prevents their bodies from drying out on land. ▼

Reptiles

A **reptile** (REHP tyl) is a vertebrate that has dry, scaly skin and lays eggs on land. Reptile eggs have tough, leathery shells. Reptiles can live in many different environments. The scales on their skin protect them from the hot Sun and from water. Reptiles can be found in hot, dry deserts or in wet rainforests. Some reptiles, such as turtles, use legs to move. Others, such as snakes, slither along the ground.

All reptiles breathe with lungs. Reptiles that spend a lot of time in water, such as crocodiles and alligators, must stick their noses out of the water to breathe.

▶ **CLASSIFY** **What are two traits of reptiles?**

Three-horned chameleons have scaly skin and three horns. ▶

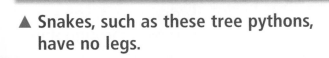

▲ Snakes, such as these tree pythons, have no legs.

◀ Tortoises, such as the one shown, and turtles both have hard shells.

Comparing Vertebrates

Vertebrates can be classified in different ways. They can be grouped by their types of body structures, where they live, the way they reproduce, or the kind of coverings on their bodies. A body covering protects an animal and helps it live in its environment. For example, birds have feathers and fish have scales.

Body Coverings

Group	Covering and Function	Example
Mammals	hair or fur protects animal, keeps body warm	giraffe hair
Birds	feathers protects animal, keeps body warm, aids flying	parrot feathers
Fish	scales protects animal, aids swimming	Garibaldi fish scales
Amphibians	moist, smooth skin protects animal, prevents drying out, some air passes through skin	blue bullfrog skin
Reptiles	dry, scaly skin protects animal, prevents drying out	chameleon skin

▶ **CLASSIFY** What are four ways that vertebrates can be classified?

Visual Summary

Vertebrates

mammals	• hair or fur • produce milk for young
birds	• feathers • hard-shelled eggs • wings
fish	• scales • gills
amphibians	• breathe with gills, then lungs • lay eggs in water
reptiles	• dry, scaly skin • leathery-shelled eggs

LINKS for Home and School

MATH **Count it Up** Human backbones are made up of many small bones called vertebrae. Humans have 33 vertebrae at birth. Some vertebrae join together as humans age. Four vertebrae combine to form one bone, and five vertebrae combine to form another bone. How many vertebrae do adult humans have?

LITERATURE **Write a Journal Entry**
Read *My Season with Penguins: An Antarctic Journal* by Sophie Webb. Use what you have learned to write a journal entry from a penguin's point of view. What are the difficulties you face? How do you meet your needs? How are you unlike other birds?

Review

❶ **MAIN IDEA** Name one trait shared by humans and fish. Name one trait that is not shared by humans and fish.

❷ **VOCABULARY** Write a sentence using the terms *backbone* and *vertebrate*.

❸ **READING SKILL: Classify** What traits make a bear a mammal?

❹ **CRITICAL THINKING: Analyze** How are young amphibians different from adult amphibians?

❺ **INQUIRY SKILL: Use Models** A toy submarine could be used to model the way a fish moves. What could you use to model the way a bird moves?

 TEST PREP
Which of the following is true of reptiles?

A. They have fur.

B. They lay eggs.

C. They have gills.

D. They can fly.

 Technology
Visit **www.eduplace.com/scp/** to find out more about vertebrates.

Which Animals Are Invertebrates?

Why It Matters...

Dragonflies, like all other insects, do not have a backbone. In fact, most of the animals on Earth do not have a backbone. Every time you hear a buzzing mosquito, pick up a wriggling earthworm, or watch a snail slowly creep along, you are observing an animal that doesn't have a backbone.

PREPARE TO INVESTIGATE

Inquiry Skill

Experiment When you experiment, you collect data that either supports a hypothesis or shows that it is false.

Materials

- earthworm
- paper towels
- water
- hand lens
- shallow pan
- black construction paper
- flashlight
- clock
- disposable gloves

Science and Math Toolbox

For step 5, review **Measuring Elapsed Time** on pages H12–H13.

Worm Work

Procedure

1 **Observe** Work in a group. Place an earthworm on a moist paper towel. Use a hand lens to examine the earthworm. **Safety:** Wear gloves and handle the earthworm gently.

2 **Record Data** In your *Science Notebook*, describe and draw the earthworm. Then make a chart like the one shown.

3 **Experiment** Line the bottom of a shallow pan with moist paper towels. Place a sheet of black construction paper so it covers one half of the pan, as shown.

4 **Predict** Predict whether the earthworm will prefer the light or dark side of the pan. Record your prediction.

5 **Experiment** Place the earthworm in the center of the pan. Hold the flashlight about 30 cm above the uncovered side of the pan, as shown. Turn on the flashlight. Wait 3 minutes. Then observe which side of the pan the worm is in. Record your observations.

6 **Experiment** Repeat step 5 three times.

Conclusion

1. **Analyze Data** Was your prediction correct?

2. **Infer** Why do you think earthworms live in soil and not on top of soil?

STEP 2

Trial	Worm found in light or dark?
1	
2	
3	
4	

STEP 3

STEP 5

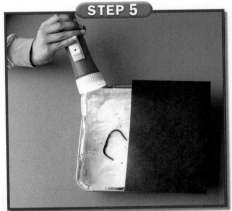

Investigate More!

Design an Experiment Find out if earthworms prefer smooth or rough surfaces. You can use sandpaper as a rough surface. Get permission from your teacher and carry out the experiment.

Invertebrates

VOCABULARY

arthropod   p. A48
invertebrate   p. A46

READING SKILL

Draw Conclusions Fill in a chart to conclude which animals in the lesson are invertebrates.

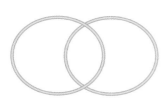

MAIN IDEA The many kinds of invertebrates can be grouped according to their traits.

Traits of Invertebrates

Most of the animals on Earth are invertebrates (ihn VUR tuh brihts). An **invertebrate** is an animal that does not have a backbone. Some types of invertebrates live on land and some types live in water.

Sponges

Sponges are animals that move very little. Their bodies are full of holes. Sponges filter tiny bits of food from the water.

Sea Stars and Sea Urchins

sea urchin

Sea stars and sea urchins have spiny body coverings. Neither animal has a head, but they both have a mouth. They move and capture food using tiny suction cups called tube feet.

sea star

Worms

Worms have soft, tube-shaped bodies with no legs, eyes, or shells. Worms live in water, in soil, or even inside other animals.

earthworm

Corals and Jellies

Corals and jellies are underwater animals. They have soft bodies, but some corals have a hard outer skeleton. They both have mouths and armlike parts called tentacles (TEHN tuh kuhlz). When food floats by, these animals use their tentacles to grab it and put it into their mouth.

coral

Snails and Squids

Snails, squid, octopus, clams, oysters, and scallops all belong to the same group called mollusks. They have soft bodies. All of these animals, except for the octopus, have a shell.

snail

▶ DRAW CONCLUSIONS   What can you conclude about an animal that has a mouth and tube feet, but no head?

Arthropods

The largest group of invertebrates is the arthropod (AHR thruh pahd) group. An **arthropod** is an invertebrate that has jointed legs, a body with two or more sections, and a hard outer covering. The hard outer covering is called an exoskeleton. An exoskeleton protects and supports the animal.

butterfly

butterflies and ants

There are several groups of arthropods. The largest group includes butterflies and ants. These insects have six legs and three body sections. They may or may not have wings.

centipede

centipedes and millipedes

Centipedes and millipedes have segmented bodies. Centipedes have one pair of legs on each segment. Millipedes have two pairs of legs on each segment.

spiders

Spiders have eight jointed legs, two body sections, jaws, and fangs. Many spiders spin webs.

spider

crabs, lobsters, and crayfish

Another group of arthropods includes crabs, lobsters, and crayfish. Many animals in this group have an exoskeleton that is very hard, like a shell.

lobster

▶ **DRAW CONCLUSIONS** Suppose you see an animal with an exoskeleton and one pair of legs on each of its body segments. Draw a conclusion about the kind of animal it is.

Visual Summary

Invertebrates

Sponges	• body with holes • move very little
Sea Stars and Sea Urchins	• hard, spiny covering • tube feet
Worms	• tube-shaped body • no legs, shells, or eyes
Jellies and Corals	• soft body • tentacles
Snails and Squids	• soft body • shell
Arthropods	• jointed legs • bodies divided into sections • hard exoskeleton

LINKS for Home and School

MATH **Use a Number Pattern** A certain centipede has 15 segments on its body. Each segment has 2 legs. Use a number pattern to find how many legs the centipede has in all.

WRITING **Story** In older times, sailors from Norway told of a sea creature called the Kraken. The Kraken was said to be more than a mile long and have tentacles strong enough to sink a ship! Today we know that these legends were probably based on a real animal, the giant squid. Choose an invertebrate and write a story about your own legendary creature.

Review

❶ **MAIN IDEA** Why are insects, lobsters, and spiders all classified as arthropods?

❷ **VOCABULARY** Write a sentence using the term *invertebrate*.

❸ **READING SKILL: Draw Conclusions** An invertebrate has a tube-like body. It does not have tentacles or legs. What can you conclude about the group it belongs to?

❹ **CRITICAL THINKING: Analyze** Lobsters and fish both have gills, but these two animals are not related. Why do you think they might both have the same body part?

❺ **INQUIRY SKILL: Experiment** Design an experiment to test this hypothesis: Ants like sugar more than they like salt.

 TEST PREP
One trait of the group containing sea stars is ___.

A. a head.

B. a body with many holes.

C. tube feet.

D. tentacles.

 Technology
Visit **www.eduplace.com/scp/** to learn more about invertebrates.

Readers' Theater

What's New at the Insect Zoo?

What's an insect and what's not? Students from the Liberty School think anything pesky that creeps, crawls, or flies is an insect. But on a visit to a nearby insectarium, they make some surprising discoveries.

Insect Zoo

Cast

Mrs. Spellman: teacher

Buzz: entomologist and insectarium guide

Carla

Raffi

Sam

Neisha

} students

Carla: So we win the school science fair, and all we get is a trip to some bug zoo? I can't believe it.

Neisha: Shhh! Here comes Mrs. Spellman.

Mrs. Spellman: *[Enters.]* Okay, kids. First we'll see some amazing insects. Then we'll go outside for a bug hunt.

Buzz: *[Enters, carrying a small branch. Buzz is energetic and speaks quickly.]* Hi kids. My name is Buzz. It's a perfect name for a bug guy, right? I was a bug collector as a kid. Now I'm an entomologist, a scientist who studies insects. Let me introduce you to Twiggy. He's a stick bug. *[Buzz shows the branch to the group.]*

Sam: All I see is a branch.

Raffi: But the top of that branch just moved! I see Twiggy now. He looks like he's part of the branch.

Mrs. Spellman: Great camouflage!

Buzz: What makes Twiggy an insect? The 6-3-2 trick for identifying insects can help you with that answer.

Sam: What trick is that?

Buzz: Insects are arthropods with *six* legs, *three* body parts and *two* antennae. If an arthropod has any other number of legs, body parts, or antennae, it's not an insect. That's the 6-3-2 trick.

Carla: Wait a minute! Spiders have eight legs, don't they? Are you saying a spider isn't an insect?

Buzz: You've got it! Spiders are arthropods, but they aren't insects. They're arachnids. They have *eight* legs, *two* body parts, and *no* antennae.

Neisha: What about these guys—the millipedes? I can't even count all their legs! *[Points to a millipede exhibit.]*

Buzz: Same deal. They're anthropods, but not insects. Millipedes have anywhere from about 100 to 400 legs. I've even heard of one type that has 750 legs! *[He reaches into the exhibit and picks up a millipede.]* Anyone want to hold Millie? She tickles when she walks on you!

Raffi: Okay!

[Buzz puts the millipede in Raffi's outstretched hand.]

Raffi: He's right! She does tickle.

▲ stick bug

▲ praying mantis

▲ ladybug

▲ butterfly

Buzz: Let's look at the praying mantis next. [*Buzz helps Raffi put the millipede back.*] It's the only insect that can swivel its head all the way around. Swiveling makes it easier for the mantis to see all of its surroundings. When another insect wanders by, the mantis grabs it and gobbles it up.

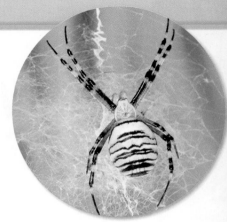

▲ spider

Sam: Yuck!

Buzz: It may sound gross to you, but the truth is, gardeners love mantises. They keep other insects from destroying plants. Now, how about that bug hunt?

Mrs. Spellman: Sure. I'll pass out the equipment.

Buzz: Okay. Let's start with a few tips. Look for insects that crawl. The best places to look are on the ground, in the grass, around trees, under rocks, and on plants.

Carla: I'm going to look for a butterfly and a ladybug!

Sam: Look! There's a butterfly in the flower garden. Let's go see it!

Neisha: We're really enjoying our insect zoo adventure. I'll bug Mrs. Spellman to let us come back soon.

▲ millipede

Sharing Ideas

1. **READING CHECK** What is a good way to identify insects?

2. **WRITE ABOUT IT** Insects such as stick bugs and praying mantises use camouflage. Why do you think this is important?

3. **TALK ABOUT IT** Discuss ways insects help farmers and gardeners.

Which Animals Lived Long Ago?

Why It Matters...

Triceratops and other dinosaurs died out millions of years ago. Scientists have learned about dinosaurs by studying their bones and footprints. They now know what dinosaurs looked like, where they lived, and even what they ate. This information helps scientists understand how dinosaurs were similar to the animals that are alive today.

PREPARE TO INVESTIGATE

Inquiry Skill

Classify When you classify, you sort objects into groups according to their properties.

Materials

- fossil A
- fossil B
- hand lens

Science and Math Toolbox

For step 2, review **Using a Hand Lens** on page H2.

Fossil Clues

Procedure

1 **Collaborate** Work with a partner. In your *Science Notebook*, make a chart like the one shown.

2 **Observe** Use a hand lens to examine fossil A and fossil B. A **fossil** is the very old remains of a plant or animal.

3 **Infer** Try to identify whether a plant or an animal made fossil A. Try to identify the parts of the living thing that fossil A came from. Record your ideas in your chart.

4 Repeat step 3 for fossil B.

Conclusion

1. **Classify** What parts of the living thing do you recognize from its fossil? What living things did they come from?

2. **Infer** What kind of environment do you think the organism that made fossil A lived in? What makes you think this?

3. **Infer** What kind of environment do you think the organism that made fossil B lived in? What makes you think this?

STEP 1

Fossil	Plant or Animal	Parts that Made Fossil
A		
B		

STEP 2

STEP 4

Investigate More!

Research Find out about fossil hunting in your state or region. What kinds of fossils have been found? What do these fossils tell about the living things of long ago?

A55

Extinct Animals

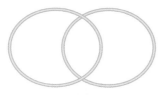

MAIN IDEA If the needs of a living thing are not met by its environment, it may not survive.

Animals of Long Ago

Dinosaurs were animals that lived millions of years ago. There were many species (SPEE-sheez) of dinosaur. A species is a group of living things that can produce living things of the same kind.

Scientists know about dinosaurs because they left behind fossils (FAHS uhlz). A **fossil** is the very old remains of a plant or animal. Scientists have found many bones, teeth, and footprint fossils of dinosaurs.

The diplodocus (dih PLAHD-uh kuhs) may have become extinct because the plants it ate died out.

Fossils help scientists understand what environments were like long ago. Fossils also help scientists learn about plants and animals that are extinct (ihk STIHNGKT). An **extinct species** is one that has disappeared. Species may become extinct if their habitat (HAB ih tat) changes. A **habitat** is the place where a plant or animal lives. If a habitat changes, the living things there may not be able to find food, water, or shelter.

Using fossil bones, scientists have made models of some extinct animals. Woolly mammoths are an extinct species. We know what they looked like from their fossils and from old drawings on the walls of caves.

Dodo (DOH doh) birds are also extinct. People destroyed the forests where dodos lived, so the birds could not find food. People also hunted dodos.

▲ The dodo had a very large body with short wings. It could not fly.

▶ **COMPARE AND CONTRAST** What is the difference between an extinct species and one that is not extinct?

Woolly mammoths were mammals that had a thick coat, curved tusks, and a large head.

A57

Extinct and Modern Animals

Many modern animals are similar to extinct animals. The woolly mammoth looked like the modern elephant. Fossils show that the rhinoceros (ry NAHS ur-uhs) and the extinct indricothere (IHN-druh koh THIHR) are related. Rhinos, like the indricothere, are mammals, eat leaves, and have feet with three toes.

The emu (EE myoo) is a large bird that cannot fly. It shares several traits with the extinct diatryma (dih A trih mah). However, fossils show that the two birds are not related.

Diatryma

A diatryma was a large bird that is now extinct. It could not fly.

Indricothere

Indricothere was the largest land mammal ever known. It was 5.5 m (18 ft) tall.

▲ An emu is a large modern bird from Australia. It cannot fly.

◄ Although the modern rhinoceros looks fierce, it eats only leaves and grass.

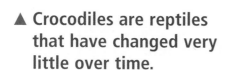

▲ Crocodiles are reptiles that have changed very little over time.

The saber-toothed cat was a fierce-looking mammal. It had two 18-cm (7-in.) teeth. Its jaws were used to rip apart the animals it hunted. It was not a fast runner because its legs were short.

This animal is not related to modern wild cats. But it has been compared to the Bengal tiger. Bengal tigers are larger and have shorter teeth and longer legs than saber-toothed cats.

▶ **COMPARE AND CONTRAST** How is a diatryma like an emu?

Extinct Crocodile

This extinct crocodile species was similar to modern crocodiles. The environment of the modern animal may be similar to that of the extinct species.

Saber-toothed Cat

Saber-toothed cats likely became extinct when the animals they ate died out.

◀ Bengal tigers and saber-toothed cats share some traits, but they are not related.

Endangered Animals

Plant and animal species are still becoming extinct. An **endangered species** (ehn DAYN jurd SPEE sheez) is one that has so few members that the entire species is in danger of becoming extinct.

Laws have been passed to protect endangered species. There have been some success stories. For example, bald eagles are returning to areas where they were once almost extinct.

▶ **COMPARE AND CONTRAST** Does a greater number of animals belong to a species that is endangered than to one that is not?

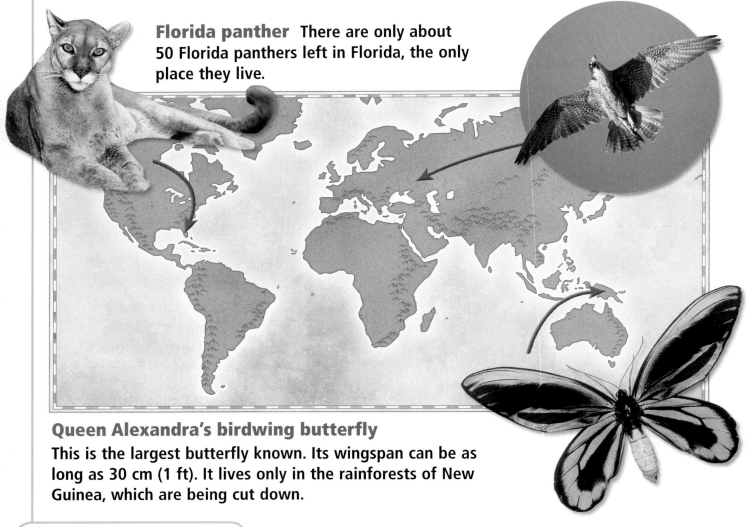

Eurasian peregrine falcon
These birds were unable to reproduce because they ate poisons used for killing insects.

Florida panther There are only about 50 Florida panthers left in Florida, the only place they live.

Queen Alexandra's birdwing butterfly
This is the largest butterfly known. Its wingspan can be as long as 30 cm (1 ft). It lives only in the rainforests of New Guinea, which are being cut down.

Visual Summary

Living things may become extinct if they cannot find food, water, or shelter.

Some modern animals resemble extinct animals. These animals may or may not be related.

Unless endangered species are protected, they could become extinct.

LINKS for Home and School

TECHNOLOGY **Recreate a Dinosaur** Scientists use computers to create pictures of dinosaurs. Choose two types of dinosaurs. Use the Internet to find computer-generated pictures of these dinosaurs. Use the pictures to create your own sketches of what these dinosaurs probably looked like.

SOCIAL STUDIES **Write a Letter** Some endangered species have been saved from extinction by people's efforts. Choose an animal on the endangered species list. Write a letter to a newspaper to tell people why that species should be saved.

Review

❶ MAIN IDEA Why might a species become extinct if its habitat is destroyed?

❷ VOCABULARY What is a fossil?

❸ READING SKILL: Compare and Contrast What is the difference between an endangered species and an extinct species?

❹ CRITICAL THINKING: Evaluate Suggest a way you could help an endangered animal from becoming extinct.

❺ INQUIRY SKILL: Classify Classify the following animals as either extinct or endangered: dodo bird, Florida panther, Eurasian falcon, saber-toothed cat, Queen Alexandra's birdwing butterfly, diatryma.

 TEST PREP All of the following can become a fossil except ___.

A. water.

B. bones.

C. teeth.

D. footprints.

 Technology Visit **www.eduplace.com/scp/** to find out more about extinct animals.

A61

No Brain, No Bones, No Problem!

A "jellyfish" is not a fish! It isn't jelly, either. In fact, jellies, to use their scientific name, are invertebrates: animals that get along fine without a spine. Everything about the giant Antarctic jelly shown here is extreme. Its bell (the rounded shape at the top) can be over three feet wide. Its tentacles can be 30 feet long. Jellies use their long tentacles to sting and catch their food.

Scientists think jellies have been around since before the dinosaurs. Not bad for an animal with no bones, no blood, no heart . . . not even a brain!

Most jellies, like these moon jellies, are much smaller than the Antarctic jelly.

Most jellies simply
float wherever
the ocean currents
take them. Others, like
the Antarctic jelly, can
move through the water
by expanding and
contracting their bells.

Vocabulary

Complete each sentence with a term from the list.

1. A sponge, a worm, a squid, and a spider is each an example of a/an _____.

2. The place where a plant or animals lives is its _____.

3. The very old remains of a living thing is a/an _____.

4. An animal that has hair or fur and produces milk for its young is a/an _____.

5. A species that is no longer found on Earth is a/an _____.

6. An animal that has gills when it is young and lungs as an adult is a/an _____.

7. An animal that has a backbone is a/an _____.

8. A vertebrate having lungs, wings, and feathers is a/an _____.

9. An animal that has jointed legs and an exoskeleton is a/an _____.

10. The series of bones that runs down the back of some animals is a/an _____.

amphibian A40
arthropod A48
backbone A36
bird A38
endangered species A60
extinct species A57
fish A39
fossil A56
habitat A57
invertebrate A46
mammal A37
reptile A41
vertebrate A36

Test Prep

Write the letter of the best answer choice.

11. Which animals have gills?

   A. reptiles
   B. fish
   C. mammals
   D. birds

12. Which of the following is a trait found in reptiles?

   A. scales
   B. wings
   C. hair
   D. feathers

13. Arthropods do NOT have _____.

   A. legs.
   B. eyes.
   C. backbones.
   D. an exoskeleton.

14. A species that has very few members is _____.

   A. extinct.
   B. endangered.
   C. doomed.
   D. a fossil.

15. **Use Models** What materials could you use to make a model of an arthropod?

16. **Classify** Invertebrates can be classified by their traits. For example, they can be grouped by whether or not they have a head, an exoskeleton, or tentacles. Choose one of these traits. List which of the following animals have that trait: coral, worm, lobster, sea star, squid, spider.

Map the Concept

Complete the concept map using the following terms.

amphibians	gills
fish	reptiles
fur	wings

17. **Apply** How do you think scientists know that saber-toothed cats ate meat?

18. **Synthesize** What might happen to the animals that live in an area where humans are moving in?

19. **Evaluate** Suppose someone tells you that carrier pigeons, an extinct species, will return to an area if its habitat is restored. Is this statement accurate?

20. **Analyze** Which animals breathe in a similar way: whales and cats or whales and sharks? Explain.

Performance Assessment

Design an Animal
Design a new mammal that lives on land. Draw and describe what your animal looks like. List what it eats. Tell about its habitat.

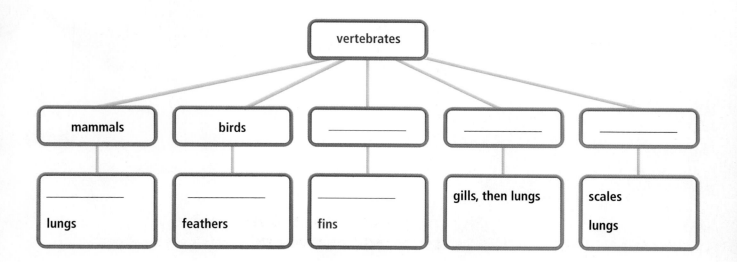

Chapter 3

Living Things Grow and Reproduce

Lesson Preview

LESSON 1

A flower, a fruit, and an insect—how do they help plants reproduce?

Read about it in Lesson 1.

LESSON 2

A turtle hatches from an egg and a caterpillar changes into a butterfly—how do the life cycles of animals compare?

Read about it in Lesson 2.

LESSON 3

Red flower or yellow flower, big dog or small dog—why do plants and animals of the same species sometimes look different?

Read about it in Lesson 3.

What Are Plant Life Cycles?

Why It Matters...

When you look outside, you probably see many types of plants. You may see huge trees or small flowers. Perhaps you see vegetables in a garden or fruits on a vine. By understanding how plants grow, people can produce the food supplies that they need.

PREPARE TO INVESTIGATE

Inquiry Skill

Observe When you observe, you gather information using your senses and tools such as hand lenses.

Materials

- clear plastic cup
- gravel
- potting soil
- pea seed
- plastic spoon
- water
- pencil
- metric ruler
- hand lens
- goggles

Science and Math Toolbox

For step 2, review **Using a Tape Measure or Ruler** on page H6.

Growing Greens
Procedure

1 **Observe** In your *Science Notebook*, make a chart like the one shown. Work with a partner. Use a hand lens to look closely at a pea seed. Draw the seed and record your observations. **Safety:** Wear goggles.

2 **Measure** Place a 2-cm layer of gravel in the bottom of a cup. Use a ruler to help you measure. Then fill the cup with soil.

3 **Experiment** Use a pencil to make a small hole in the soil. Place the pea seed in the hole and cover it with soil. Add a few spoonfuls of water. Place the cup near a sunny window.

4 **Observe** After a few days, measure the plant and observe it with a hand lens. Add water if the soil is dry. Make a drawing. Record your observations and measurements in your chart.

5 **Observe** Repeat step 4 each day for the next four days.

Conclusion

1. **Compare** Exchange charts with a partner. How are your observations similar?

2. **Predict** You have seen two stages in a plant's life cycle. What stage will you see next if your plant keeps growing?

STEP 1

Seed Growth	Drawing	Observation
Day 1		
Day 2		
Day 3		
Day 4		
Day 5		

STEP 2

STEP 3

Investigate More!

Design an Experiment Observe the inside of a tomato. Based on your observation, infer how a tomato plant grows. Design an experiment to test your idea.

Plant Life Cycles

VOCABULARY

conifer	p. A72
fruit	p. A70
life cycle	p. A70
seed	p. A70

READING SKILL

Main Idea and Details
Use a chart to show three details about the life cycle of a flowering plant.

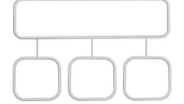

MAIN IDEA Plants have life cycles, during which they grow, reproduce, and die.

Flowering Plants

Both plants and animals have life cycles (SY kuhlz). A **life cycle** is the series of changes that a living thing goes through during its lifetime. Different living things have different life cycles. Flowering plants, such as this apple tree, have similar life cycles.

A flower, or blossom, is the part of the plant that makes fruit (froot) and seeds. A **seed** is the first stage of most plants. For a plant to produce seeds, pollen (PAHL uhn) must first move from one part of a flower to another. Pollen is a powdery material found inside flowers. The wind, insects, and other animals can move pollen.

A **fruit** is the part of the plant that contains the seeds. The apple blossoms on this tree will produce many apples. The seeds inside the apples can grow into new apple trees.

When a seed is planted in the soil it will sprout and develop into a seedling. As the seedling grows, it becomes a young tree, or sapling. When the sapling becomes an adult, the life cycle begins again. Most plants continue this cycle for many years until they die.

▶ **MAIN IDEA** What part of a flowering plant contains seeds?

Life Cycle of an Apple Tree

blossom

sapling

fruit

seedling

seed in fruit

Conifers

Not all plants have flowers. Some plants have cones instead of flowers. A **conifer** (KAHN uh fur) is a plant that makes seeds inside cones. Pine trees are conifers. Conifers use their cones to reproduce. The diagram below shows the stages in the life cycle of a conifer.

 **What is a conifer?**

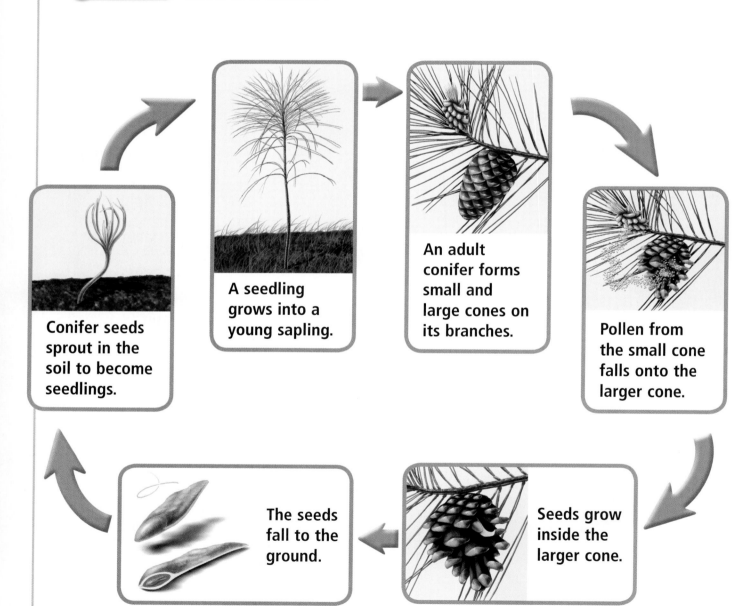

Conifer seeds sprout in the soil to become seedlings.

A seedling grows into a young sapling.

An adult conifer forms small and large cones on its branches.

Pollen from the small cone falls onto the larger cone.

The seeds fall to the ground.

Seeds grow inside the larger cone.

Visual Summary

Flowering plants grow and reproduce by making fruits and seeds from flowers.

Conifers grow and reproduce by making seeds from cones.

LINKS for Home and School

MATH **Continue the Pattern** The scale-like parts on pinecones are called bracts. Bracts are arranged in spirals. The number of bracts in each spiral follows a pattern. Look at this pattern: 1, 2, 3, 5, 8. What are the next two numbers in the pattern?

ART **Draw a Diagram** Choose a flowering plant or a conifer. Find photos or real-life examples of the plant to use as models. Draw a detailed diagram of the plant at each stage in its life cycle. Show differences in size, shape, color, and texture.

Review

❶ **MAIN IDEA** What are two things that happen during a plant's life cycle?

❷ **VOCABULARY** Write a sentence using the term *life cycle*.

❸ **READING SKILL: Main Idea and Details** List three details about the life cycle of a conifer.

❹ **CRITICAL THINKING: Analyze** How is the seed of a flowering plant different than the seed of a conifer?

❺ **INQUIRY SKILL: Observe** You see a plant that has white blossoms and small berries with seeds inside. Is the plant a flowering plant or a conifer? Explain.

✓ **TEST PREP**
A young tree is called a ___.

A. conifer.

B. seed.

C. fruit.

D. sapling.

 Technology
Visit **www.eduplace.com/scp/** to find out more about the life cycles of plants.

What Are Some Animal Life Cycles?

Why It Matters...

Like some kinds of animals, an elephant grows inside its mother's body until it is born. Other kinds of animals hatch from eggs. Some animals grow in size until they become adults. Some animals may change form. You can learn a lot about animals by studying their life cycles.

PREPARE TO INVESTIGATE

Inquiry Skill

Communicate When you communicate, you present information using words, sketches, charts, and diagrams.

Materials

- disposable gloves
- plastic container and lid
- butterfly habitat
- paper towel
- leaves
- twigs
- caterpillar food
- hand lens
- tape
- caterpillars

Caterpillar Change

Procedure

1. In your *Science Notebook*, make a chart like the one shown.

2. **Experiment** Place a folded paper towel, leaves, and twigs in a plastic container. Carefully put caterpillars and their food in the container and close the lid. **Safety:** Wear gloves and handle the caterpillars gently.

3. **Observe** Look closely at the caterpillars with a hand lens. Make a drawing and record your observations in your chart.

4. Repeat step 3 every other day for 7 to 10 days. When the caterpillars are hanging from the paper disk at the top of the container and are enclosed in a casing, remove the paper disk with the casings attached. Use tape to hang it on the wall of the butterfly habitat, as shown.

5. Repeat step 3 every other day for another 7 to 10 days.

Conclusion

1. **Compare** Compare two stages of the butterfly life cycle.

2. **Communicate** Explain how a caterpillar becomes a butterfly.

STEP 1

Drawing	Observation

STEP 3

STEP 4

Investigate More!

Research Choose an animal that lives in your area. Use library books or search the Internet to find out how the animal is born and how it changes as it grows.

Animal Life Cycles

VOCABULARY

chrysalis	p. A76
larva	p. A76
offspring	p. A78
pupa	p. A76
tadpole	p. A77

READING SKILL

Sequence
Use a chart to show the life cycle of an animal.

1	
2	
3	
4	

MAIN IDEA Different animals have different life cycles, but they are all **born, grow, reproduce, and die.**

Life Cycle of Insects

Animals follow similar stages in their life cycles. They are born, grow, reproduce, and die. But butterflies and most other insects change more than many other animals do.

The first stage in the life cycle of most insects is the egg. The second stage is a wormlike stage called the **larva** (LAHR vuh). The third stage is the pupa (PYOO puh). During the **pupa** stage, the butterfly changes into an adult. Butterflies form a case called a **chrysalis** (KRIHS uh lihs). The fourth stage is the adult. The life cycle starts again when the adult female butterfly lays eggs.

Life Cycle of a Butterfly

Egg The adult female butterfly lays eggs on a leaf.

Larva A larva, called a caterpillar, hatches from the egg.

Pupa The caterpillar becomes a pupa and makes a case called a chrysalis.

Adult An adult butterfly comes out of the chrysalis.

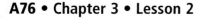

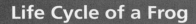

Life Cycle of a Frog

Eggs An adult female frog lays many eggs in the water.

Tadpole Tadpoles hatch from the eggs.

Young frog The tadpole becomes a small frog with legs and a tail.

Frog The adult frog has no tail and breathes with lungs.

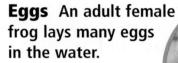
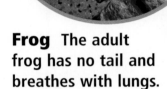

Life Cycles of Amphibians and Reptiles

Like insects, amphibians, such as frogs, change form during their life cycles. After a frog hatches from its egg, it is called a tadpole (TAD pohl). A **tadpole** lives in water and has a long tail, gills, and no legs. It looks very different from an adult frog.

Reptiles have a different life cycle from amphibians. The adult female reptile lays eggs, usually on land. After the eggs hatch, young reptiles increase in size and grow into adults. Unlike amphibians, reptiles do not change form as they grow. A young reptile looks similar to its parents.

▶ **SEQUENCE** Female insects, amphibians, and reptiles lay eggs during which stage of their life cycles?

Life Cycles of Birds and Mammals

Birds lay eggs, just as insects, amphibians, and reptiles do. Young birds have traits similar to their parents.

The offspring (AWF sprihng) of mammals grow and develop inside the bodies of adult females. **Offspring** are the living things that result when an animal reproduces. The offspring of mammals are born live. They do not hatch from eggs. At birth they look much like adult mammals. Dogs, cats, and humans grow and develop in this way.

▶ **SEQUENCE** Can a mammal be an adult as soon as it is born? Explain.

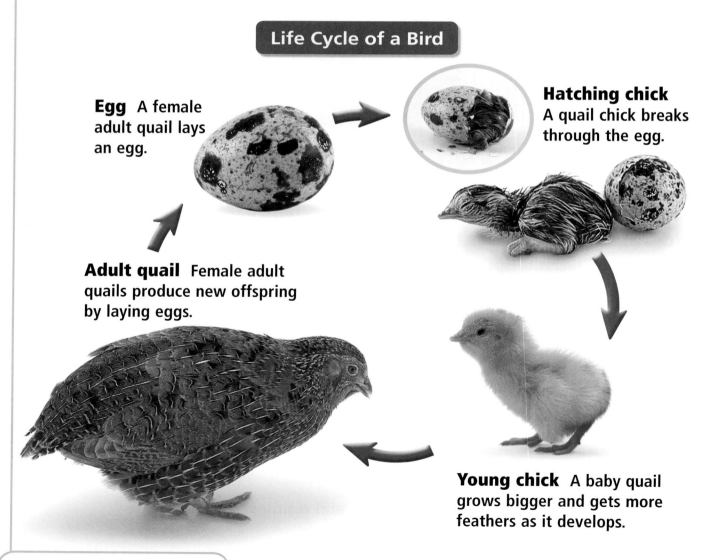

Life Cycle of a Bird

Egg A female adult quail lays an egg.

Hatching chick A quail chick breaks through the egg.

Adult quail Female adult quails produce new offspring by laying eggs.

Young chick A baby quail grows bigger and gets more feathers as it develops.

Visual Summary

Some animals are born live and other animals hatch from eggs.

↓

Animals grow in size or change into different forms as they develop.

↓

Adult animals reproduce and make new offspring.

 **LINKS** for Home and School

MATH **Calculate the Number** Suppose a farmer has 6 hens. Each hen has an equal number of eggs in her nest. When all the eggs hatch, there are 12 chicks. How many eggs did each hen have in her nest?

WRITING **Narrative** Imagine that you are a young frog. Write a narrative story about your life. Include details about how your body is changing as you grow from a tadpole into a frog.

Review

❶ **MAIN IDEA** What do the life cycles of all animals have in common?

❷ **VOCABULARY** Write a sentence using the terms *offspring* and *tadpole*.

❸ **READING SKILL: Sequence** Describe the stages in the life cycle of a bird.

❹ **CRITICAL THINKING: Analyze** Suppose that Animal A is an adult animal that hatched from an egg, once had gills, and once had a tail. What type of animal is Animal A?

❺ **INQUIRY SKILL: Communicate** Draw a diagram of the life cycle of a reptile.

✔ **TEST PREP**
An example of an animal that lays eggs but does not change forms as it grows is ___.

A. an insect.

B. an amphibian.

C. a reptile.

D. a mammal.

 Technology
Visit **www.eduplace.com/scp/** to find out more about animal life cycles.

Jane Goodall

She Dreamt of Africa. When she was a child, Jane Goodall dreamed of working with wild animals. At age 23, she left her home in England and sailed to Africa. Dr. Louis Leakey, a famous archaeologist, hired her to study chimpanzees in the Gombe forest.

At first, the chimps were afraid of Jane. She watched them from afar for months. Finally, she gained their trust. Jane spent hours observing the chimpanzees. Over time, Jane realized that chimps make and use tools, communicate with each other, and form family relationships.

In 1977, Jane founded the Jane Goodall Institute. This organization works to protect wildlife. Today, Jane travels the world, teaching people about chimpanzees and the importance of protecting the environment.

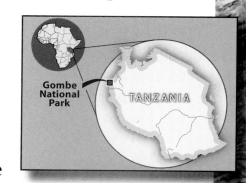

Gombe National Park is in Tanzania, a country in East Africa.

Gombe National Park is full of thick forests and steep valleys. It is a perfect environment for chimpanzees.

Baby chimps depend on their mothers for survival.

Sharing Ideas

1. **READING CHECK** How did Jane gain the chimps' trust?

2. **WRITE ABOUT IT** What are some things Jane learned about chimps?

3. **TALK ABOUT IT** Discuss the importance of protecting the African forest.

A81

How Can Living Things Vary?

Why It Matters...

These two animals look very different from one another, but they are both dogs. Living things of the same kind do not always look the same. Some may be tall and some may be short. Some may have spots and some are a solid color. Scientists study living things of the same kind to learn how they are alike and different.

PREPARE TO INVESTIGATE

Inquiry Skill

Use Numbers You use numbers when you measure, estimate, and record data.

Materials

- 4 pea pods
- index cards
- marking pen
- metric ruler

Science and Math Toolbox

For step 6, review **Making a Bar Graph** on page H3.

Peas in a Pod
Procedure

1 In your *Science Notebook*, make a chart like the one shown.

2 **Experiment** Label four index cards *A*, *B*, *C*, and *D*. Place a pea pod on each of the labeled cards.

3 **Measure** Use a ruler to measure the length of each pea pod. Record the data in your chart.

4 **Record Data** Open each pea pod. Count the number of peas in each pod. Record the data in your chart.

5 **Observe** Look at the color of the peas in each pod. Record your observations in your chart.

6 **Use Numbers** In your *Science Notebook*, copy the bar graph grid shown. Use the data in your chart to complete the graph.

Conclusion

1. **Analyze Data** Find the greatest and the least number of peas in your data. Combine this data with that of your classmates. Make a line plot to show the class data.

2. **Predict** Suppose you measured and observed four additional pea pods. Would you expect the data to be similar to the class data? Explain your answer.

STEP 1

Pea Pod	Length of Pod	Number of Peas	Color of Peas
A			
B			
C			
D			

STEP 4

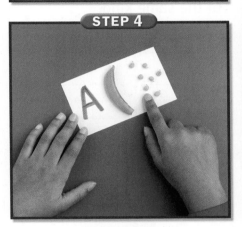

STEP 6

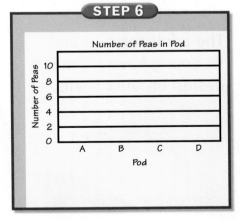

Number of Peas in Pod

Investigate More!

Research Use books or the Internet to learn about one kind of apple. Write a report about that apple type. Find out if all apples of that type have the same number of seeds.

▶ **READING SKILL**

Compare and Contrast
Use a chart to compare and contrast living things of the same kind.

Similarities and Differences

MAIN IDEA Most living things look similar to their parents. This is true because parents pass traits to their offspring.

Family Resemblance

"He has his father's eyes!" "Oh, she has her mother's smile!" You may have heard people talk about children this way. In some families, children look similar to their parents. Young plants and animals also often look like their parents. They grow to be about the same height as their parents. The color of a plant's flowers is usually similar to that of its parent plant. The color of an animal's fur is often similar to the fur of one or both of its parents.

The adult tortoise and its young have a similar design on their shells. ▼

▲ The adult and baby rabbit look very similar.

Although offspring and their parents may look similar, they do not look exactly alike. A young horse may grow to be taller or a different color than its parents. A child may have a different eye color than either parent. A grown tree may have fewer flowers or fruit than the tree from which it came.

Differences in appearance between parents and offspring are not extreme. Have you ever seen a turtle the size of a house? A turtle may grow to be larger than either of its parents. But a turtle cannot grow to be as large as a house. Similarly, a large animal, such as a giraffe, does not produce offspring that stay very small.

▲ The adult penguin and its offspring do not look exactly alike.

 **COMPARE AND CONTRAST** **Compare ways in which plants and animals may resemble their parents.**

This adult orca whale and its baby have a similar pattern on their skin.

These petunias come in many different colors.

Individuals Vary

In a crowd, you can see lots of different people—some are tall, some are short, some have blue eyes, some have brown eyes—but they are all humans. Although all people are humans, each person has different features.

There are also many differences within groups of plants and animals. One petunia flower may have red petals. Another petunia may have pink petals. A dog may have very short fur. Another dog may have so much fur that you can barely see its face! Petal color and fur length are just two examples of differences among individuals (ihn duh VIHJ oo uhlz). An **individual** is a single member of a species. Can you think of some other differences among individuals?

These are all domestic cats. Notice how different they look from one another. ▼

When living things reproduce, they pass on traits to their offspring. This explains why offspring usually look similar to their parents. Look at the three sheep shown here. The parents of the first sheep probably also had black heads. The parents of the second sheep likely had curled horns. The wooly third sheep probably had wooly parents, as well.

A living thing's environment may also affect its traits. For example, a plant that does not receive enough sunlight and water may not grow as tall as its parent plant.

Living things may also get traits from interacting with their environment. These traits are not passed on to their offspring. For example, suppose a young girl scrapes her arm. The scrape leaves a scar. She did not get this trait from her parents, and she will not pass it on to her children.

▶ **COMPARE AND CONTRAST** **Name two traits that can be different among individuals.**

▲ These animals look different, but they are all sheep.

Visual Summary

Living things usually look similar to, but not exactly like, their parents.

Individuals of the same kind usually vary in appearance.

 for Home and School

MATH **Make an Organized List** Suppose a cat has a litter of kittens. The mother cat has long, white fur and the father cat has short, black fur. What might the kittens look like? Make a list of the possible combinations of fur color and fur length.

TECHNOLOGY **Compare and Contrast** Fertilizer is a material that is put in soil to give it extra nutrients. Farmers use fertilizer as a tool for growing healthy crops. Suppose you had two plants that you gave the same amount of water and light. Imagine that you give fertilizer to only one of them. How do you think these individual plants would differ?

Review

① MAIN IDEA Why do most offspring look similar to their parents?

② VOCABULARY Define the term *individual*.

③ READING SKILL: Compare and Contrast How are the sheep on page A87 similar? How are they different?

④ CRITICAL THINKING: Evaluate You have two flowers that are the same color. Your friend says that the flowers are definitely the same species. Is this statement accurate? Explain.

⑤ INQUIRY SKILL: Use Numbers The number of petals for six flowers of the same kind are: *8, 7, 9, 7, 8, 6*. What can you infer about the number of petals usually found on this kind of flower?

✔ **TEST PREP**
Which trait can be passed on from an adult human to a child?

A. scar

B. hair color

C. sunburn

D. sprained ankle

 Technology
Visit **www.eduplace.com/scp/** to learn more about how individuals vary.

Veterinary Assistant

Do you enjoy caring for animals? As a veterinary assistant, you might help a veterinarian bandage the broken leg of a dog or calm a cat during an examination. You would also feed, water, and exercise animals. You would clean cages and exam rooms and take notes during exams. Veterinary assistants work at animal shelters, humane societies, and animal hospitals.

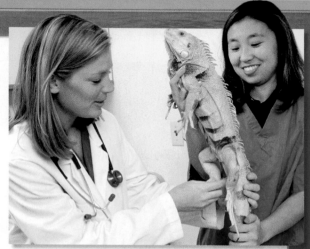

What It Takes!

- A high-school diploma.
- Courses in biology; some knowledge of medicine or dentistry

Marine Biologist

You might think marine biologists spend all their time swimming in the ocean while they study plants and animals. In fact, much of a marine biologist's work is done in a submarine or a laboratory. They use computers to track the movements of sea creatures like whales, dolphins, and sea turtles. Understanding the habits of these creatures can help scientists protect them.

What It Takes!

- A degree in biology, oceanography, or zoology
- The ability to work with computers

EXTREME Science

Mama Croc!

This mother crocodile isn't eating her baby! She's carrying it in her mouth to keep it safe from harm. Most reptiles just bury their eggs and leave them. The crocodile fiercely guards her buried eggs from other predators.

When she hears peeping from the buried eggs, she digs them out. Sometimes she even uses her huge teeth to help her babies out of their shells. After carrying them to the water, she watches over them until they are big enough to protect themselves.

This baby will grow fast—and big. Some full-grown crocodiles are longer than a family car and weigh more than a ton!

Vocabulary

Complete each sentence with a term from the list.

1. When a frog first hatches from an egg, it is called a/an _____.
2. The part of the plant that contains seeds is the _____.
3. The third stage of an insect's life cycle is the _____.
4. The series of changes a living thing goes through during its lifetime is called a/an _____.
5. A single member of a species is called a/an _____.
6. Living things that result when animals reproduce are called _____.
7. The first stage in the life cycle of most plants is the _____.
8. The case that butterflies form in their pupa stage is a/an _____.
9. A plant that grows cones is a/an _____.
10. The worm-like stage of an insect's life cycle is called the _____.

chrysalis A76
conifer A72
fruit A70
individual A86
larva A76
life cycle A70
offspring A78
pupa A76
seed A70
tadpole A77

Test Prep

Write the letter of the best answer choice.

11. Living things and their parents _____.

    A. often look similar.
    B. never look similar.
    C. are always the same size.
    D. do not interact with their environment.

12. The offspring of birds grow and develop in _____.

    A. water.   C. the adult female's body.
    B. eggs.   D. a plant.

13. Adult frogs _____.

    A. give birth to live young.
    B. live only in water.
    C. have tails.
    D. breathe with lungs.

14. The part of a plant that makes fruit and seeds is the _____.

    A. flower.   C. sapling.
    B. stem.   D. leaf.

15. **Observe** Suppose that you observe an orange tree with blossoms on it. Describe what must happen so that the tree can produce fruit and seeds.

16. **Communicate** A cottonwood leaf beetle has a life cycle that is similar to that of a butterfly. Write a paragraph to describe the life cycle of a cottonwood leaf beetle.

Map the Concept

Place the following terms in the concept map to describe the life cycle of an insect.

pupa   **egg**
adult   **larva**

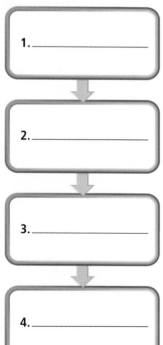

1. _____

2. _____

3. _____

4. _____

17. **Apply** Suppose you have a long-haired male dog and a long-haired female dog. You have each dog's hair cut short. If these dogs reproduce, are their puppies likely to have long hair or short hair? Explain.

18. **Evaluate** Suppose your friend says that an apple seed is similar to a frog's egg. Do you agree or disagree with this statement? Explain your answer.

19. **Synthesize** When walking in the park, you see pine cones on the ground. What can you conclude about some of the trees in that park?

20. **Analyze** How are plant life cycles and animal life cycles similar? How are they different?

Performance Assessment

Draw a Life Cycle

Choose one of the following animals: frog, hawk, mouse. Make a diagram of the life cycle of that animal. Include a drawing, label, and brief explanation of each stage of the cycle.

Write the letter of the best answer choice.

1. Which do both plants and animals have?

   A. seeds
   B. life cycles
   C. taproots
   D. larvae

2. Which pair of invertebrates are both arthropods?

   A.

   B.

   C.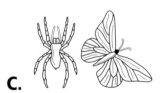

   D.

3. A carrot has a long, thick root. The veins in its leaves have many branches. Which terms describe a carrot?

   A. taproot, netted veins
   B. taproot, woody stem
   C. fibrous root, netted veins
   D. fibrous root, smooth leaves

4. All vertebrates have _____ .

   A. fur.
   B. scales.
   C. a shell.
   D. a backbone.

5. A species for which there are fewer individuals each year is said to be _____ .

   A. endangered.
   B. extinct.
   C. a fossil.
   D. reproducing.

6. Which plant stores most of its food in its stem?

A.

B.

C.

D.

7. Which shows the life cycle of a frog in the correct order?

A.

B.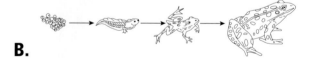

C.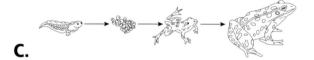

D.

8. Which is NOT needed by a seed for it to grow into a new plant?

A. soil
B. water
C. sunlight
D. wind

Answer the following in complete sentences.

9. The picture below shows a mother giraffe and her young. Describe how the two giraffes are BOTH alike and different.

10. Florida panthers are an endangered species. Explain why they are endangered.

A95

Discover!

Because dolphins and people have traits in common, they belong to many of the same animal groups. They are both vertebrates, which means they both have a backbone. They are also mammals. They produce milk for their young. Also, they use lungs to breathe. Dolphins and people are considered intelligent animals. They have large brains for their body size.

Both people and dolphins have lungs for breathing. To breathe, a dolphin swims to the surface of the water. It takes in air through an opening, called a blowhole, on the top of its head. A human breathes air through the nose and mouth.

Like most mammals, dolphins are born live. That means they don't hatch from eggs. When they are born, they look like adult dolphins, only smaller. Human babies are also born live and look like very small adults.

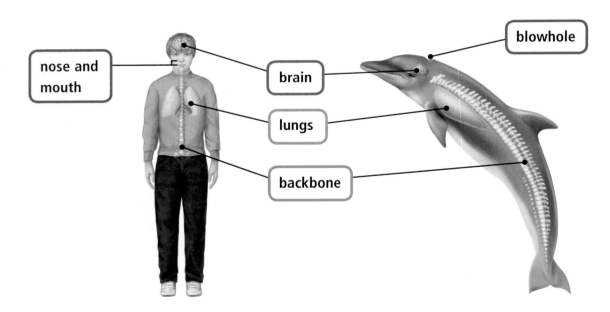

Compare a dolphin and a human. Go to **www.eduplace.com/scp/** to learn more about the features that these animals have in common.

Science and Math Toolbox

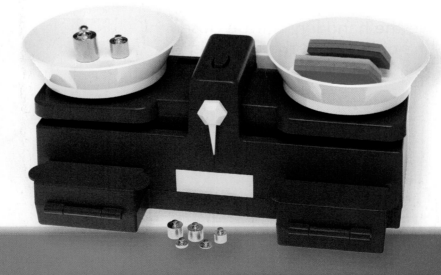

Using a Hand Lens

A hand lens is a tool that magnifies objects, or makes objects appear larger. This makes it possible for you to see details of an object that would be hard to see without the hand lens.

Look at a Coin or a Stamp

1 Place an object such as a coin or a stamp on a table or other flat surface.

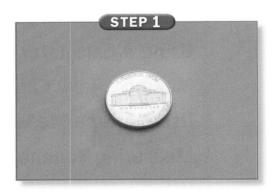

STEP 1

2 Hold the hand lens just above the object. As you look through the lens, slowly move the lens away from the object. Notice that the object appears to get larger and a little blurry.

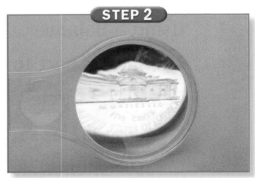

STEP 2

3 Move the hand lens a little closer to the object until the object is once again in sharp focus.

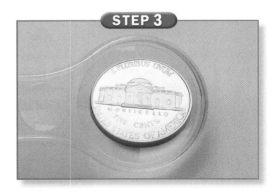

STEP 3

Making a Bar Graph

A bar graph helps you organize and compare data.

Make a Bar Graph of Animal Heights

Animals come in all different shapes and sizes. You can use the information in this table to make a bar graph of animal heights.

1. Draw the side and the bottom of the graph. Label the side of the graph as shown. The numbers will show the height of the animals in centimeters.

2. Label the bottom of the graph. Write the names of the animals at the bottom so that there is room to draw the bars.

3. Choose a title for your graph. Your title should describe the subject of the graph.

4. Draw bars to show the height of each animal. Some heights are between two numbers.

Heights of Animals

Animal	Height (cm)
Bear	240
Elephant	315
Cow	150
Giraffe	570
Camel	210
Horse	165

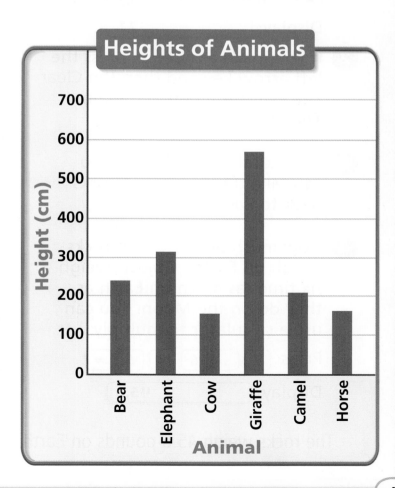

Heights of Animals

Using a Calculator

After you've made measurements, a calculator can help you analyze your data.

Add and Multiply Decimals

Suppose you're an astronaut. You may take 8 pounds of Moon rocks back to Earth. Can you take all the rocks in the table? Use a calculator to find out.

Weight of Moon Rocks	
Moon Rock	**Weight of Rock on Moon (lb)**
Rock 1	1.7
Rock 2	1.8
Rock 3	2.6
Rock 4	1.5

1 To add, press:

1 . 7 + 1 . 8 +
2 . 6 + 1 . 5 =

Display: 7.6

2 If you make a mistake, press the left arrow key and then the Clear key. Enter the number again. Then continue adding.

3 Your total is 7.6 pounds. You can take the four Moon rocks back to Earth.

4 How much do the Moon rocks weigh on Earth? Objects weigh six times as much on Earth as they do on the Moon. You can use a calculator to multiply.

Press: 7 . 6 × 6 =

Display: 45.6

The rocks weigh 45.6 pounds on Earth.

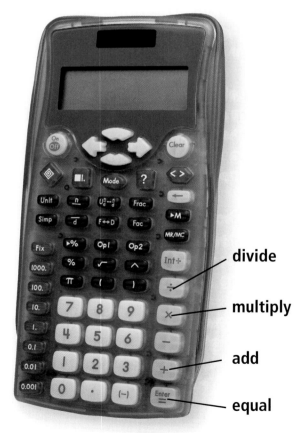

divide

multiply

add

equal

Making a Tally Chart

A tally chart can help you keep track of items you are counting. Sometimes you need to count many different items. It may be hard to count all of the items of the same type as a group. That's when a tally chart can be helpful.

Make a Tally Chart of Birds Seen

A group of bird watchers made a tally chart to record how many birds of each type they saw. Here are the tallies they have made so far.

- Every time you count one item, make one tally.

- When you reach five, draw the fifth tally as a line through the other four.

- To find the total number of robins, count by fives and then ones.

- You can use the tally chart to make a chart with numbers.

What kind of bird was seen most often?

- Now use a tally chart to record how many cars of different colors pass your school.

Birds Seen

Type of Bird	Tally
Cardinal	||
Blue jay	卌 卌 卌
Mockingbird	||||
Hummingbird	卌 ||
House sparrow	卌 卌 卌 卌	
Robin	卌 卌 ||

Birds Seen

Type of Bird	Number
Cardinal	2
Blue jay	15
Mockingbird	4
Hummingbird	7
House sparrow	21
Robin	12

Using a Tape Measure or Ruler

Tape measures and rulers are tools for measuring the length of objects and distances. Scientists most often use units such as meters, centimeters, and millimeters when making length measurements.

Use a Tape Measure

1. Measure the distance around a jar. Wrap the tape around the jar.

2. Find the line where the tape begins to wrap over itself.

3. Record the distance around the jar to the nearest centimeter.

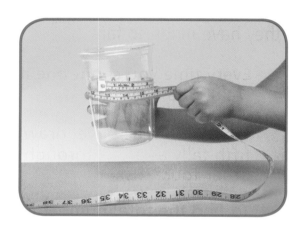

Use a Metric Ruler

1. Measure the length of your shoe. Place the ruler or the meterstick on the floor. Line up the end of the ruler with the heel of your shoe.

2. Notice where the other end of your shoe lines up with the ruler.

3. Look at the scale on the ruler. Record the length of your shoe to the nearest centimeter and to the nearest millimeter.

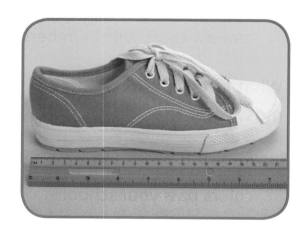

Measuring Volume

A beaker, a measuring cup, and a graduated cylinder are used to measure volume. Volume is the amount of space something takes up. Most of the containers that scientists use to measure volume have a scale marked in milliliters (mL).

Beaker
50 mL

Measuring cup
50 mL

Graduated cylinder
50 mL

Measure the Volume of a Liquid

1 Measure the volume of juice. Pour some juice into a measuring container.

2 Move your head so that your eyes are level with the top of the juice. Read the scale line that is closest to the surface of the juice. If the surface of the juice is curved up on the sides, look at the lowest point of the curve.

3 Read the measurement on the scale. You can estimate the value between two lines on the scale.

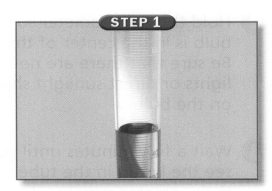

STEP 1

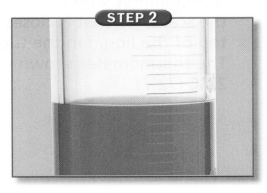

STEP 2

Using a Thermometer

A thermometer is used to measure temperature. When the liquid in the tube of a thermometer gets warmer, it expands and moves farther up the tube. Different scales can be used to measure temperature, but scientists usually use the Celsius scale.

Measure the Temperature of a Liquid

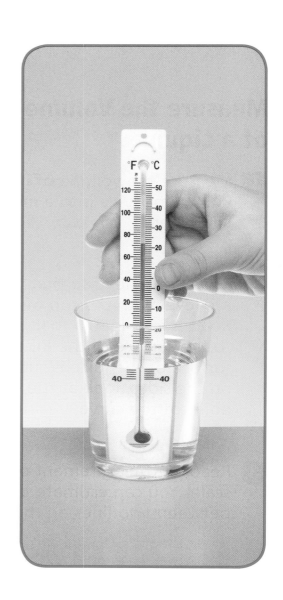

1. Half fill a cup with warm tap water.

2. Hold the thermometer so that the bulb is in the center of the liquid. Be sure that there are no bright lights or direct sunlight shining on the bulb.

3. Wait a few minutes until you see the liquid in the tube of the thermometer stop moving. Read the scale line that is closest to the top of the liquid in the tube. The thermometer shown reads 22°C (72°F).

Using a Balance

A balance is used to measure mass. Mass is the amount of matter in an object. To find the mass of an object, place it in the left pan of the balance. Place standard masses in the right pan.

Measure the Mass of a Ball

1 Check that the empty pans are balanced, or level with each other. When balanced, the pointer on the base should be at the middle mark. If it needs to be adjusted, move the slider on the back of the balance a little to the left or right.

2 Place a ball on the left pan. Then add standard masses, one at a time, to the right pan. When the pointer is at the middle mark again, each pan holds the same amount of matter and has the same mass.

3 Add the numbers marked on the masses in the pan. The total is the mass of the ball in grams.

Making a Chart to Organize Data

A chart can help you keep track of information. When you organize information, or data, it is easier to read, compare, or classify it.

Classifying Animals

Suppose you want to organize this data about animal characteristics. You could base the chart on the two characteristics listed—the number of wings and the number of legs.

1 Give the chart a title that describes the data in it.

2 Name categories, or groups, that describe the data you have collected.

3 Make sure the information is recorded correctly in each column.

Next, you could make another chart to show animal classification based on number of legs only.

My Data

Fleas have no wings. Fleas have six legs.

Snakes have no wings or legs.

A bee has four wings. It has six legs.

Spiders never have wings. They have eight legs.

A dog has no wings. It has four legs.

Birds have two wings and two legs.

A cow has no wings. It has four legs.

A butterfly has four wings. It has six legs.

Animals–Number of Wings and Legs

Animal	Number of Wings	Number of Legs
Flea	0	6
Snake	0	0
Bee	4	6
Spider	0	8
Dog	0	4
Bird	2	2
Butterfly	4	6

Reading a Circle Graph

A circle graph shows a whole divided into parts. You can use a circle graph to compare the parts to each other. You can also use it to compare the parts to the whole.

A Circle Graph of Fuel Use

This circle graph shows fuel use in the United States. The graph has 10 equal parts, or sections. Each section equals $\frac{1}{10}$ of the whole. One whole equals $\frac{10}{10}$.

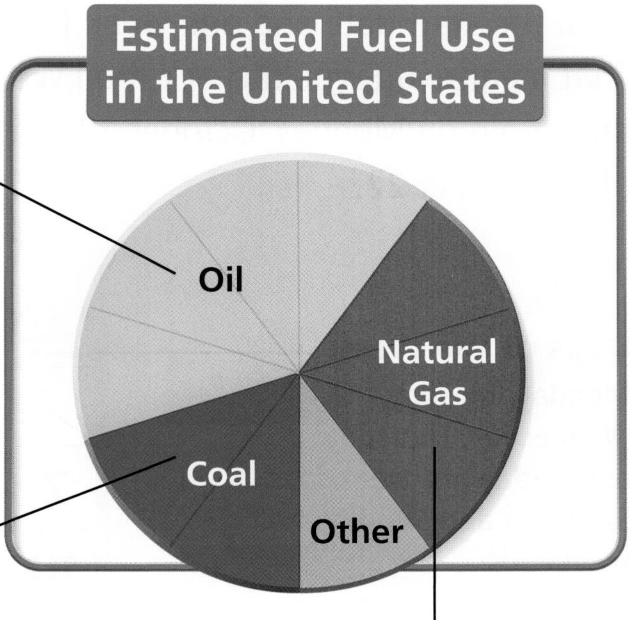

Oil Of all the fuel used in the United States, 4 out of 10 parts, or $\frac{4}{10}$, is oil.

Estimated Fuel Use in the United States

Oil
Natural Gas
Coal
Other

Coal Of all the fuel used in the United States, 2 out of 10 parts, or $\frac{2}{10}$, is coal.

Natural Gas Of all the fuel used in the United States, 3 out of 10 parts, or $\frac{3}{10}$, is natural gas.

Measuring Elapsed Time

A calendar can help you find out how much time has passed, or elapsed, in days or weeks. A clock can help you see how much time has elapsed in hours and minutes. A clock with a second hand or a stopwatch can help you find out how many seconds have elapsed.

Using a Calendar to Find Elapsed Days

This is a calendar for the month of October. October has 31 days. Suppose it is October 22 and you begin an experiment. You need to check the experiment two days from the start date and one week from the start date. That means you would check it on Wednesday, October 24, and again on Monday, October 29. October 29 is 7 days after October 22.

October

Sunday	Monday	Tuesday	Wednesday	Thursday	Friday	Saturday
	1	2	3	4	5	6
7	8	9	10	11	12	13
14	15	16	17	18	19	20
21	22	23	24	25	26	27
28	29	30	31			

Days of the Week
Monday, Tuesday, Wednesday, Thursday, and Friday are weekdays. Saturday and Sunday are weekends.

Last Month
Last month ended on Sunday, September 30.

Next Month
Next month begins on Thursday, November 1.

Using a Clock or a Stopwatch to Find Elapsed Time

You need to time an experiment for 20 minutes.

It is 1:30 P.M.

Stop at 1:50 P.M.

You need to time an experiment for 15 seconds. You can use the second hand of a clock or watch.

Start the experiment when the second hand is on number 6.

Stop when 15 seconds have passed and the second hand is on the 9.

You can use a stopwatch to time 15 seconds.

Press the reset button on a stopwatch so that you see 0:00₀₀.

Press the start button. When you see 0:15₀₀, press the stop button.

Measurements

Volume

1 L of sports drink is a little more than 1 qt.

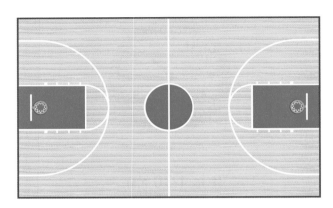

Area

A basketball court covers about 4,700 ft^2. It covers about 435 m^2.

Metric Measures

Temperature

- Ice melts at 0 degrees Celsius (°C)
- Water freezes at 0°C
- Water boils at 100°C

Length and Distance

- 1,000 meters (m) = 1 kilometer (km)
- 100 centimeters (cm) = 1 m
- 10 millimeters (mm) = 1 cm

Force

- 1 newton (N) =
  1 kilogram × 1(meter/second) per second

Volume

- 1 cubic meter (m^3) = 1 m × 1 m × 1 m
- 1 cubic centimeter (cm^3) =
  1 cm × 1 cm × 1 cm
- 1 liter (L) = 1,000 milliliters (mL)
- 1 cm^3 = 1 mL

Area

- 1 square kilometer (km^2) =
  1 km × 1 km
- 1 hectare = 10,000 m^2

Mass

- 1,000 grams (g) = 1 kilogram (kg)
- 1,000 milligrams (mg) = 1 g

Temperature

The temperature at an indoor basketball game might be 27°C, which is 80°F.

Length and Distance

A basketball rim is about 10 ft high, or a little more than 3 m from the floor.

Customary Measures

Temperature

- Ice melts at 32 degrees Fahrenheit (°F)
- Water freezes at 32°F
- Water boils at 212°F

Length and Distance

- 12 inches (in.) = 1 foot (ft)
- 3 ft = 1 yard (yd)
- 5,280 ft = 1 mile (mi)

Weight

- 16 ounces (oz) = 1 pound (lb)
- 2,000 pounds = 1 ton (T)

Volume of Fluids

- 8 fluid ounces (fl oz) = 1 cup (c)
- 2 c = 1 pint (pt)
- 2 pt = 1 quart (qt)
- 4 qt = 1 gallon (gal)

Metric and Customary Rates

km/h = kilometers per hour
m/s = meters per second
mph = miles per hour

Health and Fitness Handbook

Health means more than just not being ill. There are many parts to health. Here are some questions you will be able to answer after reading this handbook.

- How do my body systems work?
- What nutrients does my body need?
- How does being active help my body?
- How can I be safe at home?
- How can I prevent food from making me ill?

The Digestive System

Your digestive system breaks down food into materials your body can use. These materials are called nutrients.

1 Digestion starts in your mouth.
- Your teeth break food into small pieces. Saliva mixes with the food. Saliva has chemicals that break down food more.
- Your tongue pushes the chewed food into your esophagus when you swallow.

2 Food travels through the esophagus to the stomach.
- Acid and other chemicals in the stomach break down the food even more.
- The food moves to the small intestine.

3 More chemicals flow into the small intestine. They come from the liver, pancreas, and other organs.
- These chemicals finish breaking down the food into nutrients.
- The nutrients are absorbed into the blood.
- The blood carries the nutrients to all parts of the body.

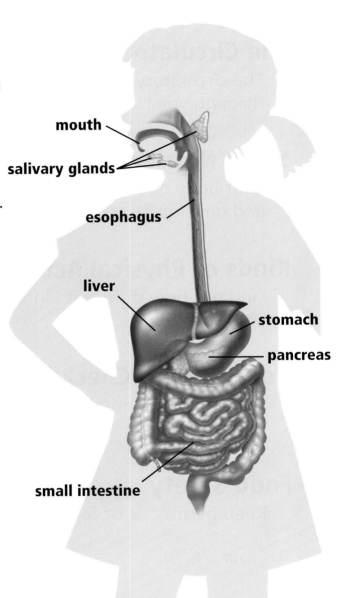

mouth

salivary glands

esophagus

liver

stomach

pancreas

small intestine

The Circulatory System

Your circulatory system moves blood through your body. There are three major parts to the circulatory system: the heart, blood vessels, and blood.

Heart Your heart has four chambers, or sections.

- The right two chambers take blood from the body and pump it to the lungs.
- There, the blood picks up oxygen and gets rid of waste.
- The left two chambers take blood from the lungs and pump it to the rest of the body.

Blood Vessels Two kinds of vessels carry blood through your body.

- **Arteries** carry blood from the heart to the body.
- **Veins** carry blood from the body to the heart.

Blood Your blood carries oxygen from your lungs to your body cells.

- Blood carries nutrients from your digestive system.
- Blood carries wastes away from the cells to organs that remove the wastes from the body.

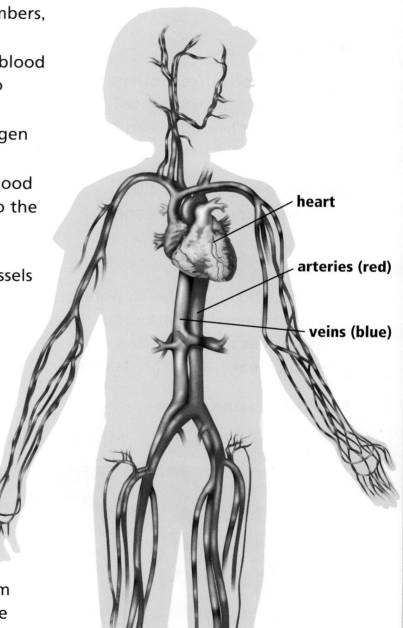

heart

arteries (red)

veins (blue)

Some Nutrients You Need

Nutrients are materials your body needs for energy and to grow. Three important nutrients are proteins, carbohydrates, and fats. Eating these nutrients in the right amount can help you stay at a healthful weight.

Proteins

Uses Your body uses proteins to build new cells and for cell activities. You need proteins to grow and develop.

Sources meat, chicken, fish, milk, cheese, nuts, beans, eggs

Fats

Uses Your body uses fat to store energy. You need to eat only a small amount of fat, because your body makes some on its own.

Sources oils and butter

Carbohydrates

Uses Carbohydrates are your body's main source of energy. Simple carbohydrates give quick energy. Complex carbohydrates give long-lasting energy. Complex carbohydrates should make up the largest part of your diet.

Sources simple carbohydrates: fruits and milk products

complex carbohydrates: whole-grain bread, cereal, pasta, potatoes

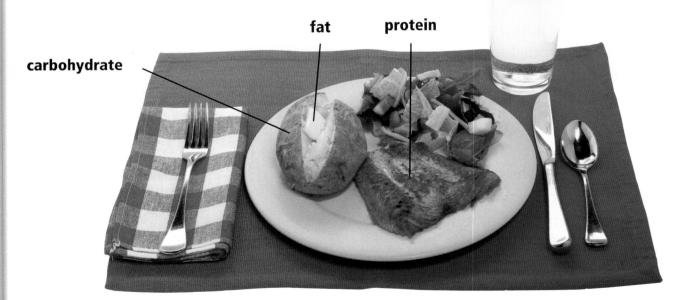

carbohydrate   fat   protein

Kinds of Physical Activity

Do you run, jump, and play every day? There are different kinds of physical activity. Each helps your body in a different way.

Endurance

Some activities help your body work hard for longer periods of time.

Activities That Build Endurance

- swimming
- jumping rope
- soccer
- in-line skating
- riding a bike
- walking fast
- basketball
- hockey

Do one of these activities for 20 to 60 minutes three to five times a week.

Flexibility

Stretching helps your muscles move smoothly.

Activities That Build Flexibility

- touching your toes
- stretching your arms
- sit and reach
- stretching your side

Do flexibility exercises two to three times a week.

Strength

These exercises make your muscles stronger. Ask an adult to show you how to do them safely.

Activities That Build Strength

- sit-ups
- push-ups
- pull-ups

Do strength training two to three days each week.

Home Safety Checklists

Most accidents happen at home. Here are some tips for staying safe.

Fire Safety

✔ Have smoke detectors. Check the batteries twice each year.

✔ Don't play with matches or candles.

✔ Only use the stove or oven if an adult is there.

✔ Have a family fire plan. Practice your plan.

Poison Safety

✔ Some chemicals and cleaners are poisons. So are some medicines. Keep them in high places away from small children.

✔ Post the phone number for Poison Control by the phone.

Kitchen Safety

✔ Never leave the kitchen while cooking.

✔ Store knives out of the reach of children.

✔ Wipe up spills immediately. Keep the floor clear of clutter.

Electrical Safety

✔ Keep electrical cords out of areas where someone could trip on them.

✔ Don't use electrical appliances near water.

✔ Unplug small appliances when you are not using them.

✔ Make sure electric cords are not damaged. They could start a fire.

Food Safety

Foods and drinks can carry germs. These germs can cause disease. Remember these four steps to keep food safe.

Clean

✔ Wash your hands before and after you cook. Wash them again if you handle raw meat, poultry, or fish.

✔ Wash all the dishes and utensils you use.

✔ Wash your hands before you eat.

Separate

✔ Keep raw meat, poultry, and fish away from other foods.

✔ Keep cooked food away from raw food.

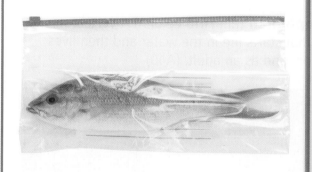

Chill

✔ Some foods need to be kept cold. Put leftovers in the refrigerator as soon as possible. This slows down the growth of germs.

✔ If you are having a picnic, keep foods in an icechest until you are ready to cook or serve them

Cook

✔ Cook food thoroughly. Cooking kills many germs.

✔ Use a thermometer to make sure foods are hot enough.

Glossary

A

adaptation (ad ap TAY shuhn) A behavior or a body part that helps a living thing survive in its environment. (B22)

alloy (AL oy) A solid solution made of at least one metal. (E55)

alternate energy resource (AWL tur niht EHN ur jee REE sawrs) An energy resource other than a fossil fuel. (C52)

amphibian (am FIHB ee uhn) A vertebrate that starts life in the water and then lives on land as an adult. (A40)

analyze data (AN uh lyz DAY tuh) To look for patterns in collected information that lead to making logical inferences, predictions, and hypotheses.

aquatic habitat (uh KWAT ihk HAB ih tat) A place where organisms live in or on water. (B60)

arthropod (AHR thruh pahd) An invertebrate that has jointed legs, a body with two or more sections, and a hard outer covering. (A48)

ask questions (ask KWEHS chuhz) To state orally or in writing questions to find out how or why something happens, which can lead to scientific investigations or research.

asteroid (AS tuh royd) A piece of rock that orbits the Sun. (D48)

atmosphere (AT muh sfihr) The layers of air that cover Earth's surface. (D14)

axis (AK sihs) An imaginary line through the center of an object. (D68)

B

backbone (BAK bohn) A series of bones that runs down the back of a vertebrate animal. (A36)

behavior (bih HAYV yur) The way that an organism typically acts in a certain situation. (B22)

bird (burd) A vertebrate that has feathers, lungs, wings, and two legs and lays eggs that have hard shells. (A38)

C

carnivore (KAHR nuh vawr) An animal that eats only other animals. (B51)

cell (sehl) The smallest and most basic unit of a living thing. (A8, B45)

chemical change (KEHM ih kuhl chaynj) A change in matter in which one or more new kinds of matter form. (E23)

chemical property (KEHM ih kuhl PRAHP ur tee) A property that describes how matter can react with other kinds of matter. (E22)

chrysalis (KRIHS uh lihs) The hard case an insect forms to protect itself during the pupa stage. (A76)

classify (KLAS uh fy) To sort objects into groups according to their properties or order objects according to a pattern.

climate (KLY miht) The average weather conditions in an area over a long period of time. (D25)

collaborate (kuh LAB uh rayt) To work as a team with others to collect and share data, observations, findings, and ideas.

communicate (kah MYOO nuh kayt) To explain procedures or share information, data, or findings with others through written or spoken words, actions, graphs, charts, tables, diagrams, or sketches.

community (kuh MYOO nih tee) A group of plants and animals that live in the same area and interact with each other. (B15)

compare (kuhm PAIR) To observe and tell how objects or events are alike or different.

condensation (kahn dehn SAY shuhn) The change of state from gas to liquid. (D7)

condense (kuhn DEHNS) To change state from gas to liquid. (E15)

conifer (KAHN uh fur) A plant that makes seeds inside cones. (A72)

conservation (kahn suhr VAY shuhn) The safe-keeping and wise use of natural resources. (C62)

constellation (kahn stuh LAY shuhn) A group of stars that forms a pattern shaped like an animal, person, or object. (D86)

consumer (kuhn SOO mur) An organism that gets energy by eating other living things. (B51)

core (kohr) The innermost layer of Earth. (C14)

crater (KRAY tur) A bowl-shaped dent caused when an object from space strikes the surface of a planet or a moon. (D78)

crest (krehst) The highest point of a wave. (F15)

crust (kruhst) The thin, outermost layer of Earth. (C14)

D

data (DAY tuh) Information collected and analyzed in scientific investigations. (S3)

direction (di REHK shuhn) The path an object follows. (F83)

dissolve (dih ZAHLV) To mix completely with another substance to form a solution. (E52)

distance (DIHS tuhns) A measure of length. (F82)

E

earthquake (URTH kwayk) A sudden movement of large sections of Earth's crust. (C21)

ecosystem (EE koh SIHS tuhm) All of the living and nonliving things that exist and interact in one place. (B10)

electric circuit (ih LEHK trihk SUR kiht) A path around which electric current can flow. (F29)

electric current (ih LEHK trihk KUR uhnt) The flow of charged particles. (F28)

endangered species (ehn DAYN jurd SPEE sheez) A species that has so few members that it may soon become extinct. (A60)

energy (EHN ur jee) The ability to cause change. (B7)

environment (ehn VY ruhn muhnt) All the living and nonliving things that surround and affect an organism. (A24, B10)

equator (ih KWAY tuhr) An imaginary line around the Earth, halfway between the North Pole and the South Pole. (D26)

erosion (ih ROH zhuhn) The process of carrying weathered rock from one place to another. (C31)

evaporate (ih VAP uh rayt) To change state slowly from liquid to gas. (E15)

evaporation (ih vap uh RAY shuhn) The change of state from liquid to gas. (D7)

experiment (ihks SPEHR uh muhnt) To investigate and collect data that either supports a hypothesis or shows that it is false while controlling variables and changing only one part of an experimental setup at a time.

extinct species (ihk STIHNGKT SPEE sheez) A species that has disappeared. (A57)

filter (FIHL tur) A device or material that traps some substances and allows others to pass through. (E44)

fish (fihsh) A vertebrate that lives in water and uses gills to take oxygen from water. (A39)

food chain (food chayn) The path that energy takes through a community as one living thing eats another. (B50)

force (fawrs) A push or a pull. (F73)

fossil (FAHS uhl) The very old remains of a plant or animal. (A56, C22)

fossil fuel (FAHS uhl FYOO uhl) A fuel that forms over a very long time from the remains of plants and animals. (C50)

freeze (freez) To change state from liquid to solid. (E15)

friction (FRIHK shuhn) A force that occurs when one object rubs against another object. (F45)

fruit (froot) The part of a plant that contains the seeds. (A70)

full moon (ful moon) The phase of the Moon when all of the Moon's sunlit side faces Earth. (D75)

gas (gas) Matter that has no definite shape and does not take up a definite amount of space. (E7)

geothermal energy (jee oh THUR muhl EHN ur jee) Heat from inside Earth. (C52)

gravity (GRAV ih tee) A force that pulls objects toward each other. (F74)

habitat (HAB ih tat) The place where an organism lives. (A57, B32)

heat (heet) The flow of thermal energy from warmer objects to cooler objects. (F42)

herbivore (HUR buh vawr) An animal that eats only plants. (B51)

humus (HYOO muhs) The decayed remains of plants and animals. (C32)

hydroelectric energy (hy droh ih LEHK trihk EHN ur jee) Electricity made from the force of moving water. (C52)

hypothesize (hy PAHTH uh syz) To make an educated guess about why something happens.

igneous rock (IHG nee uhs rahk) Rock that forms when melted rock from inside Earth cools and hardens. (C18)

inclined plane (ihn KLYND playn) A simple machine made up of a slanted surface. (F94)

individual (ihn duh VIHJ oo uhl) A single member of a species. (A86)

infer (ihn FUR) To use facts and data you know and observations you have made to draw a conclusion about a specific event based on observations and data. To construct a reasonable explanation.

inner planets (IHN ur PLAN ihts) The four planets closest to the Sun: Mercury, Venus, Earth, and Mars. (D46)

invertebrate (ihn VUR tuh briht) An animal that does not have a backbone. (A46)

kinetic energy (kuh NET ihk EHN ur jee) Energy of motion. (F8)

landform (LAND fawrm) A part of Earth's surface that has a certain shape and is formed naturally. (C8)

larva (LAHR vuh) The second, worm-like stage in an insect's life cycle. (A76)

latitude (LAT ih tood) The distance north or south of the equator. (D26)

leaf (leef) The part of a plant that collects sunlight and gases from the air and uses them to make food for the plant. (A8)

lever (LEHV ur) A simple machine made up of a stiff arm that can move freely around a fixed point. (F91)

life cycle (lyf SY kuhl) The series of changes that a living thing goes through during its lifetime. (A70)

light (lyt) A form of energy that you can see. (F58)

liquid (LIHK wihd) Matter that takes the shape of its container and takes up a definite amount of space. (E7)

magnify (MAG nuh fy) To make an object appear larger. (D38)

mammal (MAM uhl) A vertebrate that has hair or fur, produces milk for its young, and breathes air with its lungs. (A37)

mantle (MAN tl) The thick, middle layer of Earth. (C14)

mass (mas) The amount of matter in an object. (E9)

matter (MAT ur) Anything that has mass and takes up space. (E6)

measure (MEHZ uhr) To use a variety of measuring instruments and tools to find the length, distance, volume, mass, or temperature using appropriate units of measurement.

melt (mehlt) To change state from solid to liquid. (E15)

metamorphic rock (meht uh MAWR fihk rahk) Rock that forms when other rock is changed by heat and pressure. (C18)

mineral (MIHN ur uhl) A material that is found in nature and that has never been alive. (C16)

mixture (MIHKS chur) Matter that is made up of two or more substances or materials that are physically combined. (E35)

moon (moon) A small, rounded body that orbits a planet. (D45)

motion (MOH shuhn) A change in the position of an object. (F72)

natural resource (NACH ur uhl REE sawrs) A material from Earth that is useful to people. (C42)

netted veins (NEHT tihd vaynz) Veins that branch out from main veins. (A16)

new moon (noo moon) The phase of the Moon when the Moon is not visible from Earth because none of its sunlit side faces Earth. (D75)

nonrenewable resource (nahn rih NOO uh buhl REE sawrs) A natural resource that is in limited supply and that cannot be replaced or takes thousands of years to be replaced. (C44)

nutrient (NOO tree uhnt) A substance that living things need in order to survive and grow. (A7)

observe (UHB zuhrv) To use the senses and tools to gather or collect information and determine the properties of objects or events.

offspring (AWF sprihng) The living thing made when an animal reproduces. (A78)

omnivore (AHM nuh vawr) An animal that eats both plants and animals. (B51)

orbit (AWR biht) To move in a path, usually around a planet or a star. (D44)

ore (AWR) Rock that contains metal or other useful minerals. (C42)

organism (AWR guh nihz uhm) Any living thing. (B8)

outer planets (OW tur PLAN ihts) The four planets farthest from the Sun: Jupiter, Saturn, Uranus, and Neptune. (D47)

parallel veins (PAR uh lehl vaynz) Veins that run in straight lines next to each other. (A16)

phases of the Moon (FAYZ ihz uhv thuh moon) The different ways the Moon looks throughout the month. (D76)

physical change (FIHZ ih kuhl chaynj) A change in the size, shape, or state of matter. (E14)

physical property (FIHZ ih kuhl PRAHP ur tee) A characteristic of matter that can be measured or observed with the senses. (E7)

pitch (pihch) How high or low a sound seems. (F18)

planet (PLAN iht) A large body in space that orbits a star. (D44)

plant (plant) A living thing that grows on land or in the water, cannot move from place to place, and usually has green leaves. (A6)

polar climate (POH lur KLY miht) A climate with long, cold winters and short, cool summers. (D27)

pollution (puh LOO shuhn) 1. Any harmful material in the environment. (B34); 2. The addition of harmful materials to the environment. (C60)

population (pahp yuh LAY shuhn) All the organisms of the same kind that live together in an ecosystem. (B14)

potential energy (puh TEHN shuhl EHN ur jee) Stored energy. (F8)

precipitation (prih sihp ih TAY shuhn) Any form of water that falls from clouds to Earth's surface. (D8)

predict (prih DIHKT) To state what you think will happen based on past experience, observations, patterns, and cause-and-effect relationships.

producer (pruh DOO sur) An organism that uses energy from the Sun to make its own food. (B51)

pulley (PUL ee) A simple machine made up of a rope fitted around a fixed wheel. (F93)

pupa (PYOO puh) The third stage of an insect's life cycle, during which it changes into an adult. (A76)

R

record data (rih KAWRD DAY tuh) To write (in tables, charts, journals), draw, audio record, video record, or photograph, to show observations.

recycle (ree SY kuhl) To collect old materials, process them, and use them to make new items. (C62)

reflect (rih FLEHKT) To bounce off. (F60)

refract (rih FRAKT) To bend. (F61)

renewable resource (rih NOO uh buhl REE sawrs) A natural resource that can be replaced by nature. (C44)

reproduce (ree proh DOOS) To make new living things of the same kind. (A26)

reptile (REHP tyl) A vertebrate that has dry, scaly skin and lays eggs on land. (A41)

research (rih SURCH) To learn more about a subject by looking in books, newspapers, magazines, CD-ROMs, searching the Internet, or asking science experts.

resource (REE sawrs) A material found in nature that is useful to organisms. (B15)

revolve (rih VAHLV) To move in a path around an object. (D68)

root (root) The part of a plant that takes in water and nutrients and provides support for the plant. (A8)

rotate (ROH tayt) To turn on an axis. (D68)

S

satellite (SAT l yt) Any object that revolves around a planet or other larger object. (D74)

scientific inquiry (sy uhn TIHF uhk ihn - KWIHR ee) The ways scientists ask and answer questions about the world, including investigating and experimenting. (S4)

screw (skroo) A simple machine made up of an inclined plane wrapped around a column. (F95)

sedimentary rock (sehd uh MEHN tuh ree rahk) Rock that forms when sediment is pressed together and hardens. (C18)

seed (seed) The first stage in the life cycle of most plants. (A70)

simple machine (SIHM puhl muh SHEEN) A tool with few parts that makes work easier. (F90)

soil (soyl) The loose material that covers much of Earth's surface. (C30)

solar energy (SOH lur EHN ur jee) The energy that comes from the Sun and provides Earth with light and heat. (B44)

solar system (SOH lur SIHS tuhm) The Sun and the planets, moons, and other objects that orbit the Sun. (D45)

solid (SAHL ihd) Matter that has a definite shape and takes up a definite amount of space. (E7)

solution (suh LOO shuhn) A special kind of mixture in which two or more substances are so evenly mixed that the separate parts cannot be seen. (E52)

space probe (spays prohb) A craft that explores outer space carrying instruments, but not people. (D58)

speed (speed) A measure of how fast or slow an object is moving. (F84)

star (stahr) A ball of hot gases that gives off light and other forms of energy. (D84)

stem (stehm) The part of a plant that holds up the leaves and carries water and nutrients through the plant. (A8)

substance (SUHB stuhns) A single kind of matter that has certain properties. (E34)

Sun (suhn) The nearest star to Earth. (D44)

tadpole (TAD pohl) The stage in a frog's life cycle when it hatches from the egg and has a long tail, gills, and no legs. (A77)

technology (tek NAHL uh jee) The tools people make and use and the things they build with tools. (S11)

telescope (TEHL ih skohp) A tool that makes distant objects appear larger and sharper. (D38)

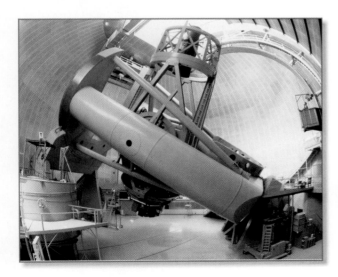

temperate climate (TEHM pur iht KLY miht) A climate with warm or hot summers and cool or cold winters. (D26)

temperature (TEHM pur uh chur) The measure of how hot or cold something is. (D16, F50)

terrestrial habitat (tuh REHS tree uhl HAB ih tat) A place where organisms live on land. (B62)

thermal energy (THUR muhl EHN ur jee) The energy of moving particles in matter. (F42)

thermometer (thur MAHM ih tur) A tool that is used to measure temperature. (F50)

tropical climate (TRAHP ih kuhl KLY miht) A climate that is very warm and wet for most of or all of the year. (D26)

trough (trawf) The lowest point of a wave. (F15)

use models (yooz MAHD lz) To use sketches, diagrams or other physical representations of an object, process, or idea to better understand or describe how it works.

use numbers (yooz NUHM burz) To use numerical data to count, measure, estimate, order, and record data to compare objects and events.

use variables (yooz VAIR ee uh buhlz) To keep all conditions in an experiment the same except for the variable, or the condition that is being tested in the experiment.

vein (vayn) A tube that carries food, water, and nutrients throughout a leaf. (A16)

vertebrate (VUR tuh briht) An animal that has a backbone. (A36)

vibrate (VY brayt) To move back and forth quickly. (F16)

volume (VAHL yoom) 1. The amount of space that matter takes up. (E9); 2. How loud or soft a sound seems. (F19)

water cycle (WAH tur SY kuhl) The movement of water between the air and Earth as it changes state. (D8)

water vapor (WAH tur VAY pur) Water in the form of an invisible gas. (D6)

wave (wayv) A movement that carries energy from one place to another. (F14)

weather (WEHTH ur) The condition of the atmosphere at a certain place and time. (D16)

weathering (WEHTH ur ihng) The breaking up or wearing away of rock. (C30)

wedge (wehj) A simple machine made up of two inclined planes. (F95)

wheel and axle (hweel and AK suhl) A simple machine made up of a small cylinder, or axle, attached to the center of a larger wheel. (F92)

work (work) The movement of an object by a force. (F90)

Index

Permission Acknowledgements

Excerpt from Deer, Moose, Elk, and Caribou, by Deborah Hodge, illustrated by Pat Stevens. Text Copyright © 1998 by Deborah Hodge. Illustrations copyright © 1998 by Pat Stevens. Reprinted by permission of Kids Can Press, Ltd., Toronto. Excerpt from The Wump World, by Bill Peet. Copyright © 1970 by Bill Peet. Reprinted by permission of Houghton Mifflin Company. Excerpt from Thunder and Lightning from How & Why Stories: World Tales Kids Can Read & Tell, by Martha Hamilton and Mitch Weiss. Copyright © 1999 Martha Hamilton and Mitch Weiss. Reprinted by permission of Marian Reiner on behalf of August House Publishers, Inc. Excerpt from Thunderstorms What is a Thunderstorm? from Hurricanes Have Eyes But Can't See, by Melvin and Gilda Berger. Copyright © 2003, 2004 by Melvin and Gilda Berger. Reprinted by permission of Scholastic Inc. Excerpt from Freckle Juice, by Judy Blume. Text copyright © 1971 by Judy Blume. Reprinted with the permission of Harold Ober Associates Incorporated and Simon & Schuster Books for Young Readers, an imprint of Simon & Schuster Children's Publishing Division. Excerpt from Freckle Juice, by Judy Blume. Text copyright © 1971 by Judy Blume. Reprinted with the permission of Simon & Schuster Books for Young Readers, an imprint of Simon & Schuster Children's Publishing Division and Harold Ober Associates Incorporated.

Cover

(Toucan) © Steve Bloom/steve-bloom.com. (Rainforest bkgd) © Bill Brooks/Masterfile. (Back cover toucan) Masterfile Royalty Free (Spine) Natural Visions/Alamy.

Photography

Unit A Opener: Doug Perrine/Innerspace Visions/Seapics.com. A1 Michael S. Nolan/AGE Fotostock. A3 (tr) Burke/Triolo/Brand X/Picturequest. (br) Karl & Kay Amman/Bruce Coleman Inc. (lc) Grant Heilman Photography. A2–A3 (bkgd) Photo 24/Brand X. A6–A7 (b) Charles O'Rear/Corbis. (t) Terry W. Eggers/Corbis. A8 (r) © Phil Degginger/Color Pic, Inc. (c) © Dwight Kuhn. A9 (r) © Dwight Kuhn. (bc) Microfield Scientific LTD/Science Photo Library/Photo Researchers, Inc. A10 Melanie Acevedo/Botanica/Getty Images. A11 (tr) Peter Chadwick/DK Images. (br) Dave King/DK Images. A10–A11 (b) David M. Schleser/Nature's Images, Inc./Photo Researchers, Inc. A13 (t) Charles O'Rear/Corbis. (c) © Phil Degginger/Color Pic, Inc. A14 (bl) Judy White/Garden Photos. A14–A15 (bkgd) Roger Ressmeyer/Corbis. A16 (r) Neil Fletcher & Matthew Ward/DK Images. (l) Matthew Ward/DK Images. A17 (bl) Andrew McRobb/DK Images. (br) Nigel Cattlin/Holt Studios Int./Photo Researchers, Inc. (tl) Norman Owen Tomalin/Bruce Coleman, Inc. (tc) Neil Fletcher & Matthew Ward/DK Images. (tr) Ian O'Leary/DK Images. A18 (br) © Dwight Kuhn. (tl) ChromaZone Images/Index Stock Imagery. (tr) © E.R. Degginger/Color Pic, Inc. (bl) John Kaprielian/Photo Researchers, Inc. A19 (t) Matthew Ward/DK Images. (c) ChromaZone Images/Index Stock Imagery. (b) © Dwight Kuhn. A21 (cr) Dave King/DK Images. A20–A21 (bkgd) Bruce Dale/National Geographic/Getty Images. A22 (bl) © E.R. Degginger/Color Pic, Inc. A22–A23 (bkgd) Natural Selection Stock Photography. A24 (bl) Francois Gohier/Francois Gohier Nature Photography. (r) Michael & Patricia Fogden/Corbis. A25 (r) Michael Fogden/DRK Photo. (l) © E.R. Degginger/Color Pic, Inc. A26 (br) Angelo Cavalli/Superstock. (tl) © Dwight Kuhn. (bl) © Dave Kuhn/Dwight Kuhn Photography. A27 (c) Michael Fogden/DRK Photo. (t) Michael & Patricia Fogden/Corbis. (b) Angelo Cavalli/Superstock. A33 (t) A. & S. Carey/Masterfile. (c) Geoff Dann/DK Images. (b) Chip Clark/Smithsonian Museum of Natural History. A32–A33 (bkgd) Bios/Peter Arnold. A34 (bl) George Shelley/Masterfile. A35 (picture card, snake) GK Hart/Vikki Hart/Photodisc/Getty Images. (picture card, bird) GK Hart/Vikki Hart/Photodisc/Getty Images. A34–A35 (bkgd) Miep Van Damm/Masterfile. A36 Ernest Janes/Bruce Coleman, Inc. A37 (t) Tom & Dee Ann McCarthy/Corbis. (b) © E.R. Degginger/Color Pic, Inc. A38 (c) Mervyn Rees/Alamy Images. (b) Tom Tietz/Stone/Getty Images. (tl) Photri. A39 (bkgd) Jeff Greenberg/Photo Edit, Inc. A39 (tr) Jeff Hunter/The Image Bank/Getty Images. (t) Brandon Cole Marine Photography/Alamy Images. (c) Franklin Viola/Animals Animals. A40 (b) Frank Krahmer/Bruce Coleman, Inc. (tr) Gregory G. Dimijian/Photo Researchers, Inc. A41 (t) C.K. Lorenz/Photo Researchers, Inc. (b) Sidney Bahrt/Photo Researchers, Inc. (c) Gerry Ellis/Minden Pictures. A42 (tc) Daniel Zupanc/Bruce Coleman, Inc. (b) Art Wolfe/Getty Images. (c) Jeff Rotman/Photo Researchers, Inc. (t) Art Wolfe/Photo Researchers, Inc. (bc) Corbis. A44 (bl) Larry West/Bruce Coleman, Inc. A44–A45 (bkgd) Gary Meszaros/Dembinsky Photo Associates. A46 (c) I & K Stewart/Bruce Coleman, Inc. (bl) Christy Gavitt/DRK Photo. (br) Jett Britnell/DRK Photo. A47 (c) Carl Roessler/Bruce Coleman, Inc. (t) Grant

Heilman Photography. (b) Bryan Reinhart/Masterfile. **A48** (t) Gail Shumwav/Bruce Coleman, Inc. (bc) Joe Mcdonald/DRK Photo. (b) Jane Burton/Bruce Coleman, Inc. (tc) Alex Kerstitch/Bruce Coleman, Inc. **A52** (cr) Donald Mammoser/Bruce Coleman, Inc. (cl) Kim Taylor/Bruce Coleman, Inc. (br) Bob Jensen/Bruce Coleman, Inc. (bl) Adam Jones/Dembinsky Photo Associates. **A53** (bl) Justin Sullivan/Reportage/Getty Images. (tr) H. Zettl/Masterfile. **A57** (b) Jonathan Blair/Corbis. (tr) George Bernard/Science Photo Library/Photo Researchers. **A58** (cr) Fritz Prenzel/Animals Animals. (b) ZSSD/Minden Pictures. **A59** (t) Colin Keates/DK Images. (b) Art Wolfe/Photo Researchers, Inc. **A60** (lc) Superstock. (cr) Johnathan Gale/Photographer's Choice/Getty Images. (br) Colin Keates/DK Image. **A61** (t) George Bernard/Science Photo Library/Photo Researchers, Inc. (c) Fritz Prenzel/Animals Animals. (b) Superstock. **A67** (t) William Manning/Corbis. (c) © Dwight Kuhn. (b) Renee Stockdale/Animals Animals. **A66–A67** (bkgd) © Thomas Wiewandt/www.wildhorizons.com. **A71** (bkgd) Martin Ruegner/Imagestate/Alamy Images. (t) MaryAnn Frazier/Photo Researchers, Inc. (cr) Stephen P. Parker/Photo Researchers, Inc. (br) Foodfolio/Alamy Images. (bl) © Dwight Kuhn. (lc) Nigel Cattlin/Holt Studios International Ltd./Alamy Images. **A73** MaryAnn Frazier/Photo Researchers, Inc. **A74–A75** Mitch Reardon/Stone/Getty images. **A76** (lc) Robert Pickett/Alamy Images. (m) © Raymond Mendez/Animals Animals-Earth Scenes. (b) © Neo Edmund/Shutterstock. (mr) © Randy M. Ury/Corbis. **A77** (t) Stephen Dalton/Photo Researchers, Inc. (r) George Bernard/Photo Researchers Inc. (b) George Bernard/Photo Researchers, Inc.

(l) Stephen Dalton/Photo Researchers, Inc. **A78** (tl) Jane Burton/DK Images. (tr) Jane Burton/DK Images. (cr) Jane Burton/DK Images. **A78** (br) Jane Burton/DK Images. (bl) Cyril Laubscher/DK Images. **A81** (bl) Anup Shah/Nature Picture Library. **A80–A81** (bkgd) Michael Nichols/National Geographic. **A82–A83** Ricky John Molloy/Stone/Getty Images. **A84** (r) Ernest A. Janes/Bruce Coleman, Inc. (l) Bios/Peter Arnold. **A85** (tr) Johnny Johnson/DRK Photo. (b) Jeff Foott/Bruce Coleman, Inc. **A86** (br) Rolf Kopfle/Bruce Coleman, Inc. (tl) Richard Shiell. (bl) Ulrike Schanz/Photo Researchers, Inc. (bc) Jacana/Photo Researchers, Inc. **A87** (bl) Carolyn A. McKeone/Photo Researchers, Inc. (br) John Daniels/Bruce Coleman, Inc. (tr) Piet Opperman. (cr) Colin Seddon/Nature Picture Library. (br) Steven David Miller Nature Picture Library. **A88** (t)Bios/Peter Arnold. (b)Richard Shiell. **A89** (bkgd) Doug Perrine/Seapics.com. (tr) Kaz Mori/The Image Bank/Getty Images. Unit B Opener: Dan Guravich/Guravich Photgraphy. **B1** Dan Guravich/Guravich Photgraphy. **B3** (t) Ron Stroud/Masterfile. (tc) Gary Vestal/Stone/Getty Images. (bc) Eric Soder/Photo Researchers, Inc. (b) John Foster/Masterfile. **B2–B3** (bkgd) Alan Carey/Alan and Sandy Carey Photography. **B4** (bl) Gary R. Zahm/DRK Photo. **B4–B5** (bkgd) James Randklev/The Image Bank/Getty Images. **B8** (tl) © Inga Spence/Indexstock. (bl) Clive Streeter/DK Images. **B9** (br) Burke/Triolo Productions/FoodPix. (tr) Michael Wickes/Bruce Coleman, Inc. (bl) Jeff L. Lepore/Photo Researchers, Inc. **B11** (tl) © Inga Spence/Indexstock. **B12** (bl) Photri. **B12–B13** (bkgd) Eric Von Weber/Stone/Getty Images. **B14** (bc) John Hawkins; Frank Lane Picture Agency/Corbis. (cl) Stephen J

Krasemann/DRK Photo. (bc) Joe McDonald/Corbis. (cr) W. Perry Conway/Corbis. **B15** (cr) M. Loup/Peter Arnold. (t) Jim Brandenburg/Minden Pictures. **B14–B15** (bkgd)John Shaw/Bruce Coleman, Inc. **B16** (tr) Dale Wilson/Masterfile. (b) Konrad Wothe/Minden Pictures. **B17** (tr) Richard Laird/Taxi/Getty Images. (b) Clark James Mishler. **B18** Dominique Braud/Dembinsky Photo Associates. **B19** (t) Jim Brandenburg/Minden Pictures. (b) Dominique Braud/Dembinsky Photo Associates. (c) Konrad Wothe/Minden Pictures. **B20** (br) Michael & Patricia Fogden/Corbis. **B20–B21** (bkgd) Jack Dermid/Photo Researchers. **B22** (r) Scott Camazine/Photo Researchers, Inc. (l) Susanne Danegger/Photo Researchers, Inc. **B23** (b) Wayne Lynch/DRK Photo. (t) Howard Miller/Photo Researchers, Inc. **B26** (tl) Tom Bean/DRK Photo. (b) Jeffrey Rotman, Photo Researchers, Inc. **B30–B31** (bkgd) Steve Holt/Stockpix.com. **B32** Stan Osolinski/Dembinsky Photo Associates. **B34** B. Blume/UNEP/Peter Arnold. **B35** (b) B. Blume/UNEP/Peter Arnold. (t) Stan Osolinski/Dembinsky Photo Associates. **B41** (t) Jacana/Photo Researchers, Inc. (c) © Gary Meszaros/Photo Researchers, Inc. (b) Michael Aw/Lonely Planet Images/Getty Images. **B40–B41** (bkgd) Jeff Foott/Nature Picture Library. **B42** (bl) Michael Fogden/DRK Photo. **B42–B43** (bkgd) J. A. Kraulis/Masterfile. **B44–B45** © Jeff Greenberg/The Image Works, Inc. **B46** (c) Michael P. Gadomski/Photo Researchers, Inc. (br) Wayne Lankinen/DRK Photo. (bl) Joe McDonald/Corbis. (tl) © E.R. Degginger/Color Pic, Inc. (tr) Ariel Skelley/Corbis. **B47** © Jeff Greenberg/The Image Works, Inc. (c) Michael P. Gadomski/Photo Researchers, Inc. (b) Joe McDonald/Corbis. **B48** (bl) Satoshi Kuribayashi/OSF/DRK Photo.

F57, F62, F70, F71, F72, F73, F75, F77, F79, F88, F89 © HMCo./Ken Karp Photography. F90, F91, F92, F93 © HMCo./Lawrence Migdale Photography. F94 © HMCo./Ken Karp Photography. F96 © HMCo./Lawrence Migdale Photography. F97 © HMCo./Ken Karp Photography.

Illustration

A6–A7 Jeff Wack. A12 Phil Wilson. A13 Phil Wilson. A31 Robert Schuster. A36 Joel Ito. A50–A51 Shane McGowan. A54 Patrick Gnan. A54–A55 Patrick Gnan. A56 Patrick Gnan. A58 Patrick Gnan. A59 Patrick Gnan. A60 Karen Minot. A72 Michigan Science Art. A73 Michigan Science Art. A80 Joe LeMonnier. A96 Sharon and Joel Harris. B07 Tracy Sabin. B10 Michael Maydak. B11 Michael Maydak. B24–B25 Michael Maydak. B33 Richard Orr. B35 Richard Orr. B52–B53 Michael Maydak. B55 Michael Maydak. B60–B61 Richard Orr. B62–B63 Richard Orr. B64 Richard Orr. B72 Sharon and Joel Harris. C06 Steve Durke. C08–C09 Steve McEntee. C10 Joe LeMonnier. C11 (t) Steve Durke. (c) Steve McEntee. (b) Joe LeMonnier. C15 Steve McEntee. C22 Joel Dubin. C24–C25 Doug Bowles. C26 Joe LeMonnier. C32 Steve Durke. C33 Steve Durke. C63 Robert Schuster. C64 Argosy Publishing. C65 Argosy Publishing. C72 Phil Wilson. D08–D09 Michael Saunders. D11 Michael Saunders. D14 Peter Bull. D18 Joe LeMonnier. D19 Joe LeMonnier. D20 © Chris Sheban. D26 Joe LeMonnier. D28 Joe LeMonnier. D33 Joe LeMonnier. D44–D45 Bob Kayganich. D48 Bob Kayganich. D75 Argosy Publishing. D76 Argosy Publishing. D79 Argosy Publishing. D86 Argosy Publishing. D87 Argosy Publishing. D96 Patrick Gnan. E14 Argosy Publishing. E15 Patrick Gnan. E21 Patrick Gnan. E48–E49 Tracy Sabin. E96 Patrick Gnan. F16–F17 Argosy Publish-ing. F22–F23 Maryn Roos. F24 Sharon and Joel Harris. F24–F25 (bkgd) Maryn Roos. F37 Argosy Publishing. F51 Promotion Studios. F52 Argosy Publishing. F74 George Baquero. F75 Argosy Publishing. F91 George Baquero. F92 George Baquero. F93 George Baquero. F94 George Baquero. F95 George Baquero. F104 Linda Lee Mauri.

Extreme Science

A28–A29 © Robert & Linda Mitchell/Mitchell Photography. A29 (t) © Michael Durham/Durham Photography. (b) © Dwight Kuhn/Dwight Kuhn Photography. A62–A63 © Norbert Wu/Minden Pictures. A62 (b) © John C. Elk III. A90–A91 © Roger De La Harpe/Animals Animals. A91 (b) Anup Shah/naturepl.com. B36–B37 © Frans Lanting/Minden Pictures. B36(b) © Shawn Gould. B66–B67 © Brandon Cole. B66 (b) © Peter Parks/Image Quest 3-D. C34–C35 © Y. Arthus–Bertrand/Altitude. C66–C67 AP/Wide World Photos. C67 (t) Jose Azel/Aurora. D30–D31 NOAA. D60–D61 Courtesy The W.M. Keck Observatory. D60 (b) © Forrest J. Egan. D61 (b) Simon Fraser/Science Photo Library. D90–D91 © Stefan Seip. D91 (t) © COR-BIS. E26–E27 Terry Rishel/© Dale Chihuly Studio. E27 (t) Mark Wexler/© Dale Chihuly Studio. E57–E58 © Pete Saloutos. F34–F35 © Stephen Dalton/NHPA. F34 (b) © Barry Mansell/nature-pl.com. F64–F65 © Tony Crad-dock/Science Photo Library. F65 (b) © Dr. Peter Moore/Science Photo Library. F98–F99 © Chris Trotman/NewSport/CORBIS.

Nature of Science

PHOTOGRAPHY: (Rhinoceros Beetle) © Stephen Dalton/NHPA. S1 © Jim Cummins/Corbis. S2-3 Dan Brumbaugh/AMNH Center for Biodiversity and Conservation. S3 (r) Tim Calver/Discovery Channel Online. S4-5 © Doug McCutch-eon/LGPL/Alamy Images. S5 (r) © HMCo./Joel Benjamin Pho-tography. S6-7 © Andreas Hart/OKAPIA/Photo Researchers, Inc. S7 (r) © HMCo./Ed Imaging. S8-9 © HMCo./Joel Benjamin Photography. S10-1 Jonathan Santos. S11 © Corbis. S12 (l) HMCo./Studio Montage. S12-3 © The Image Bank/Getty Images. S14-5 Peter Pinnock/ImageState/PictureQuest. S15 (r) © HMCo./Ed Imaging.

Health and Fitness Handbook

ASSIGNMENT: H21 (m) (b), H23 (tl) © HMCo./Joel Benjamin. H18, H19 © HMCo./Coppola Studios Inc. PHOTOGRAPHY: H16 Nick Clements/Taxi/Getty Images. H21 Comstock. H23 (br) Brian Smith. ILLUSTRATION: H18–H19 Kate Sweeney.